The Visions of Sor María de Agreda

The Visions
of
Sor María de Agreda

Writing Knowledge and Power

Clark Colahan

THE UNIVERSITY OF ARIZONA PRESS

Tucson & London

The University of Arizona Press

Copyright © 1994 by Arizona Board of Regents.

All rights reserved

♾ This book is printed on acid-free, archival-quality paper.

Manufactured in the United States of America

98 97 96 95 94   5 4 3 2 1

Library of Congress Cataloging in Publication Data

Colahan, Clark A. (Clark Andrew), 1945–
The visions of Sor Mariá de Agreda : writing knowledge and power /
by Clark Colahan.
    p.   cm.
Includes bibliographical references and index.
ISBN 0-8165-1419-4 (alk. paper)
    1. María de Jesús, de Agreda, sor, 1602–1665.   2. Mysticism—
Spain—History—17th century.   3. Women mystics—Spain—Biography.
    4. Franciscans—Spain—Biography.   5. Nuns' writings—History and
criticism.   I. Title.
BV5095.M28C65   1994
71'.97302—dc20
    [B]   94-9569
                                                              CIP

British Library Cataloguing in Publication Data

A catalogue record for this book is available from the British Library.

The University of New Mexico Press has generously given permission to use
extended quotations from *Fray Alonso de Benavides' Revised Memorial of 1634*,
edited by Hodge, Hammond, and Rey. Copyrighted 1945.

Contents

Acknowledgments

I hope these pages will make a difference to the following friends, who for a dozen years have helped me to understand a Spanish nun's vision:

For Mark María de Agreda Carrico, the young Albuquerque carpenter through whom I first learned of Sor María and met the founder of a religious order inspired by Sor María's writings—a strong contender in the Saint Joseph soulmate competition, Irish-American division.

For the Mother Superior and the sisters at the Conceptionist convent in Agreda, Spain, who welcomed and assisted me, allowing me, after obtaining due episcopal approbation, to enter the cloistered walls, examine the library, and there sort papers on the coffin containing the uncorrupted remains of Sor María's mother.

For Father Celestino Ruipérez, the person heading the efforts for Sor María's canonization, who with graciousness and warmth accompanied me on my visit inside the convent.

For José Antonio Pérez Rioja, Madrid scholar and retired director of the Soria Cultural Center, author of the best bibliographic study on Sor María, who opened up to me his home, his files, and his contacts all over Spain.

For Joaquín Pérez Villanueva, director of Spain's Center for Inquisitorial Studies, who shared hours of highly informed conversation on Agredan subjects.

For Angel Uribe, scholarly Franciscan friar who helped me sort out the location of Agredan documents in Spanish archives.

For Antonio Vázquez Fernández, Professor of Religious Psychology at the Pontifical University of Salamanca, Spain, whose encouragement and ideas helped me bridge the gap between an obscure religious topic and a subject full of broad human appeal.

For Alfred Rodriguez, former teacher, winner of the Letras de Oro literary prize, confidant and unfailing help, reader of *The Mystical City of God*, who coauthored my first published essay on Sor María.

For Thomas Steele, Society of Jesus, English professor, whose lectures, writings, and friendship taught me much about Hispanic Catholicism in the Southwest.

For John Kessell, New Mexican historian and expert in the region's colonial period, who shared his knowledge and his thoughts on Sor María's life.

For the late Ruth Anthony, the distinguished feminist Hispanist, who when she was Ruth El-Saffar, read my manuscript, offered encouragement, and made efforts on behalf of its publication.

For Roberta Davidson, fellow literature teacher at Whitman College and director of the Gender Studies Program there, who worked with me on connections between Hispanic and English women writers like Sor María.

For Carmen Rasines, my "Spanish mother," who read the manuscript of the original Spanish-language version of the study and told me there were too many big words in it.

For Barbara Coddington, art museum curator, patient editor, my partner in marriage, who read one of the penultimate versions of the book and made me see what was not yet clear.

For Joseph Weber, Santa Fe composer, who read the first thing I ever wrote about Sor María and turned it into a successful opera.

For Michele Larsson, Santa Fe choreographer, who worked with Joe and made an opera into a stunning opera-ballet.

For María Teresa Alvarez, director of the documentary on Sor María for Televisión Española, who chose me to be the scholarly expert and allowed me to decide what to film in New Mexico.

For Vincenta Colahan, my mother, who told me not to give up, to write it all again in English, when the Spanish-language version of this study could not find a publisher in a newly socialist Spain sick of Franco's force-fed Catholicism.

For my eight-year-old son Benjamin, faithful companion who, when he was not quite a year old, "bilocated" to Spain with me on my sabbatical dedicated to the book.

And finally, for Sor María de Agreda, from whom I learned a lot about myself and who used to wake me up nights to tell me to get back to work on her story.

1

Introduction

Through the kindness of the generous and loving mercy of the Most High, the light of the Lord, coming out to meet me as I entered life through the door of rational thought, showed me the beauty and importance of truth so that I might love it and by that love be urged on to reach it.[1]

In the Hispanic world the fame of the Venerable Sor María de Agreda (1602–1665) is considerable and has been constructed on a three-part base: She is known, above all, as the author of *The Mystical City of God*, a voluminous biography of the Virgin Mary and detailed chronicle of her relationship with the human race, based on Sor María's revelations from the Virgin herself; second, she was the friend and advisor of Felipe IV, the king of Spain, with whom she exchanged hundreds of letters; and third, she was the miraculous missionary said to have carried out a "bilocation" to New Mexico and Texas during the Age of Discovery. Sor María was believed to have personally taken the gospel to the Indians without ever once leaving her hometown in the province of Soria by conventional means. In the American Southwest, Sor María's bilocation has been remembered ever since in the legend of the Lady in Blue.

Sor María still provokes surprise and polemic. Above all, it has been her great book that has brought her either respect bordering on adoration or smiles of amused disdain. Published some 250 times and translated into a dozen languages since its posthumous appearance in 1670, *The Mystical City of God* split Europe into Agredists and anti-Agredists.[2] Efforts toward Sor María's canonization continue today, and as recently as twenty years ago, the Spanish government actively supported such efforts. Rulers as diverse as the liberal Carlos III and the reactionary Francisco Franco took special interest in helping her cause at the Vatican. Yet in spite of this celebrity status, several of her significant writings have never been published, nor is there a literary study of her work as a whole. Why?

An assembly convoked by the Sorbonne in 1696 foreshadowed *The Mystical City of God's* reception by the intellectual world. A minority of the scholars were not adverse to the fervent Marian devotion of the time and voted to accept the work as free of theological errors and probably the result of authentic supernatural inspiration. The majority, however, more oriented toward rationalism and the imminent Age of Enlightenment, rejected the work as patently deluded and possibly a somewhat fraudulent attempt by the Franciscan order in Spain to build a case for the much-debated theological hypothesis of the Immaculate Conception, which affirms that the Virgin Mary was born free of original sin. The indignant response of other universities, including many in Spain, was not long in coming.

Indeed, the book was part of such vehement controversy over the Immaculate Conception—into which Catholics at that time poured so much partisan energy—that in 1616 and 1622, two popes felt compelled to issue prohibitions of discussion of the subject.[3] In 1675, Ippolito Maracci, a Marian enthusiast who refused to obey the ban on preaching, was excommunicated. In France, oaths were taken to defend the Virgin's honor, and there was brawling in the streets on her account.[4]

At the root of the emotion were two issues, both related to the Reformation and the church's response to it: first, whether or not the Virgin is Christ's equal in glory and power, and second, whether traditions developed over the centuries within the church are as valid as the biblical record. As we shall see, *The Mystical City of God* portrays the Virgin as a full-fledged partner of her son, co-Redeemer of the World, knowing and doing the same things. Saint Jean Eudes, Sor María's exact contemporary, similarly raised the Virgin nearly to the Godhead in affirming that she "was an exact counterpart to Jesus: He [God] would give this Virgin Mother to us. And as the Son is the figure of his substance . . . and the perfect image of the Divinity . . . so also Mary should bear a perfect resemblance to him."[5] This identification can be understood in light of the fact that more and more throughout the Middle Ages, Mary had come to be thought of as the maternal, forgiving intercessor for sinners with God the Father, feared as a strict judge. In this role, she is the intermediary between God and individuals, just as Jesus, in the New Testament, is the Lamb of God, the sacrifice that reconciles God and mankind.

In the movement toward self-direction that characterized the Renaissance and Reformation, the Virgin offered an acceptable avenue of personal access to the spiritual power at the heart of Christianity. Over the course of fifteen hundred years, the church had grown increasingly codified and institutionalized, insulating its members from the immediate, uplifting experience of divine revelation. While Protestants embraced a belief in divine guidance for individuals in their own readings of the Bible, Catholics found emotional sanctuary in both Mary and mysticism. Especially for Catholic women, living within a religion overwhelmingly dominated by men, what could have been more natural than turning for solace and inspiration not to a rigid institution ruled by severe padres, but instead to an inner world warmed by an understanding and all-powerful mother?

The especially vigorous defense in Spain of the doctrine of the Immaculate Conception is related also to that country's self-concept as the most stalwart defender of the Counter-Reformation. The Jesuits, whose order was founded in Spain in 1534, were guided by the finding of the Spanish-dominated Council of Trent that traditions of the faithful were to be held in equal honor with the biblical text. Reacting to the Protestant insistence on adhering to Scripture, and in particular to the pointed rejection of the doctrine due to its absence there, the Jesuits insistently defended the Immaculate Conception as one of those extratextual truths that the church had recovered through later reasoning and revelation. For this reason, its very absence from the Bible was a spur to its defense.[6]

Almost equally important, at least in Spain, was support for the belief by the Franciscans, within whose order the Immaculate Conception had been formulated in the thirteenth century. Marian devotion in general was part of the Franciscan emphasis on Christ's human nature. Stories of the holy family, often dramatized, figured importantly in their missionary programs, both to the southern part of the country, where there was a strong Muslim tradition, and to the New World. The province of Almería, in the mountainous outback of Granada, Islam's most persistent cultural enclave on the Spanish peninsula and the most stubborn enemy of Franco's campaign to impose orthodoxy in the 1940s, still retains the Franciscan influence in place names such as San José and Pozo del Fraile, "The Friar's Well." In California, the eighteenth-century Franciscan missions had names like Purísima, "Immaculate," and Nuestra Señora la Reina de Los Angeles, "Our Lady Queen of Angels."

In England, the Age of the Reformation brought an emphatic end to this sort of adoration of the Virgin, a practice associated with allegiance to Rome instead of the new Church of England's independence and the Protestants' reliance on Scripture. A striking example is "England's Nazareth," a house built about 1130 to the dimensions of the holy family's house, said to have been revealed by the Virgin to a woman in Walsingham. For the remainder of the Middle Ages, it was a center of pilgrimage and, reputedly, continuing miracles. As a young man, Henry VIII supported England's Nazareth generously, but in 1538 he had the shrine dismantled and the miracle-working statue burned.[7] Devotion to the Virgin and the saints came to be thought of as part of the cluster of practices centered on externals—relics, pilgrimages, rituals—that replaced real inner spirituality with what until recently has been called "popery." On the other hand, the individual's right, or even duty, to rely on a personal interpretation of Scripture encouraged freedom of thought, creating an intellectual climate in which skepticism, the basis of modern science, took root early. This anti-mystical bias in connection with the cult of the Virgin can be seen clearly today in the Anglo-American *Catholic Encyclopedia*, whose article on "private revelation" makes a point of warning the reader to be wary of extravagant claims about the Virgin such as those made by Sor María de Agreda.

In nineteenth-century Spain, in contrast, *The Mystical City of God* remained a source of pride, even a point of honor, among conservatives, especially among those having Franciscan sympathies. The distinguished novelist and professor of comparative literature Emilia Pardo Bazán, although not a conservative in most matters, was an enthusiast and published a condensation of the book. She wrote: "[Sor María] deserves to be considered one of our classics on the basis of the purity, strength and elegance of her style; among our theologians on the basis of her abundance and depth of doctrine; among our philosophers on the basis of her rigorous logic and mental vigor. In her time learned bishops and grave doctors felt confused and amazed, unable to make sense of the fact that an uneducated female, whose only schooling had been through meditation, could follow securely in the steps of Saint Thomas and Duns Scotus."[8]

Liberals, on the other hand, who liked to identify their politics with the century's positivistic brand of science, were more careful. When Sor María cropped up in the context of their historical or literary research, they usually limited their analysis to remarking that her popular impact was, deservedly, in decline.[9] To these writers, it never would have occurred to bring out a first edition of new works by a writer with such a radically supernatural epistemology, especially in light of the strange experiences attributed to her, the very sort of superstitious extravagances against which the encyclopedist Father Feijoo had fought in the eighteenth century. Their intellectual adversaries (and that is the word to use in the context of the divided Spain that was bled by civil wars in the last century as well as the twentieth) were equally unlikely to dig around in Sor María's secondary works, though for entirely different reasons. Conservatives probably feared that a comparison of her other writings and the controversial biography, of which they were so proud but others so scornful, would point to human sources of inspiration and methods of composition. The Holy Scriptures themselves, as Christian traditionalists saw with alarm, were being subjected to the same kind of treatment by the new biblical scholarship.

This is the reason so much of the present bibliography on Sor María has been produced either by Franciscans with an unshakable pride in their extraordinary nun or by historians of a thoroughgoing skepticism, with many in both groups being non-Spaniards. In the United States, understandably, scholars have concentrated not on her writings but on her legend—its origin, historical references to tribes who retained the memory of having seen and heard her, and how much or how little truth there might be at its core. Prior to the 1960s, the nature of Sor María's mystical legend—which makes her personality and writings valuable for an understanding of the culture of the Hispanic Southwest and, in a broader context, Christianity's image of the maternal aspect of God—ran counter to the direction of progress. For many, it was only another of the quaint, romantic artifacts of the Spanish Southwest, emotional nonsense surviving in a generally scientific view of the world. However, as the country's ideology has struggled toward pluralism, and the history of women, ethnic groups, and peripheral regions has gained recognition, Sor María's distinctive presence has attracted more attention.

Her importance for women's studies is clear. Sor María's spiritual and imaginative life, the resonances it has called forth perennially from her readers, and their place within comparative literature and religion are complemented by her historical life. Like that of her model, Teresa de Avila, Sor María provides an extraordinary example of a woman overcoming restrictions. Although she never left the town where she was born and never lived anywhere except her parents' house or the convent her mother founded, still she became a famous missionary to the American Southwest—became that in her mind and the minds of her king, church, companions, and the very Indians she had so wished to help. Though Sor María was unable to go to court to counsel the king, he went to her, and then for years he sought her advice in active correspondence. Though limited by her gender in opportunities for formal study, Sor María wrote not only influential letters, memoirs, and collections of prayers, but even a little geography and cosmology before undertaking her monumental biography of the Virgin. In all of this, she has much to offer as an exemplar of a woman successfully working for recognition within a narrowly prescribed social role and its accompanying discourse while ultimately managing to subvert them.

The subversion culminated in Sor María's life of the Virgin, who over the centuries has been one of the most revered women in the history of European civilization. The biography, while a creation of the imagination, has offered thousands and thousands of readers a role model who is not passive, but active, powerful, even all-knowing, and who was of fundamental importance in the history of the church and mankind in general. The traditional paternalistic view of the Virgin, in keeping with the little space she receives in the biblical account of the life of her son, urged women to keep quiet and to think of themselves primarily as self-sacrificing mothers, enclosed within their own long-suffering hearts, pierced swordlike by the Virgin's seven traditional sorrows taken from the Gospels. In fact, statues of Mary with real swords piercing her chest in a cluster over the heart are still frequently found in Hispanic Catholic churches.

This justification for denying women leadership roles was made use of explicitly, to cite one example, by a churchman working to diminish the influence of María de Santo Domingo, a reforming nun of the early sixteenth century.[10] But after the publication of *The Mystical City of God*, the Spanish church, especially the Franciscans, looked to the book's energetic image of the Virgin on more than one occasion as a positive example to be followed, even by men, in areas of active endeavor, as her influence on Fray Junípero Serra and the missionaries to California clearly shows.

One would think, then, that a person seeking a deeper understanding of Sor María's legend and of what her life and work have to say in more than theological terms could turn to Spain, where her perennially and internationally read literature would have been studied and the reasons for its hold on so many people's imagination articulated. But no, Spanish critics have shown no interest, but rather an apparent unwillingness to taint themselves with a work popular with the wrong sort of readers. Of the nation's internationally recognized writers of the last two centuries, only the feminist Pardo Bazán has argued for Sor María's inclusion in the canon of Spanish literature.[11]

Famous novelists in the liberal camp, Benito Pérez Galdós, for example, repeatedly have ridiculed the stories surrounding her. Juan Valera—urbane, ironical, and critical of the impact of the mystical tradition on Spanish life—in *Pepita Jiménez* described the false priestly vocation of the male protagonist as a wish to be another Sor María de Agreda. In his 1977 novel, *Fragments of Apocalypse*, Torrente Ballester, who edited Sor María's correspondence with Felipe IV, sounds a distorted echo of her reports to the king about the afterlife of his dead wife and son when Ballester's modern protagonist makes weekend trips to hell to bring back politically useful information.[12] The scoffers have apparently carried the day in Spain; in a 1989 conference celebrating the five-hundredth anniversary of Sor María's own Conceptionist order, nuns from the León convent, not far from Agreda, told me *The Mystical City of God*, once intensively studied in the order, was a book they had not read and about which they had been warned to be alert for errors in case they should.

This sort of disdain has meant that the artistic and psychological elements that have kept Sor María's epic in publication for centuries still remain unexamined. One would like to point out diplomatically to Spanish scholars that *Paradise Lost* has suffered less from this kind of ideological prejudice, allowing the English-speaking world to recognize the important human value of its own seventeenth-century epic set in a grandiose religious frame.

Given that since 1975 the "two Spains" have made an effort to listen to each other in the political forum, the moment may be right for a fresh, open-minded look into such highly charged corners in the history of the national spirit. Moreover, the growing acceptance of women's studies means that the importance for Spain of an intuitive, visionary woman can now be more easily recognized. And finally, Sor María's case is of interest because she reflects Renaissance Spain's view of the expanding geographical world, a view that was part of the impulse leading to Spanish exploration and colonization.

Two important books on Sor María in the last twenty-five years already have taken steps toward a less polarized, more conciliatory approach to the long-stewing "caso Agreda." The first was the excellent biography by the English historian Sir Thomas Kendrick, which combines the advantages of good archival documentation with careful methodology and his perspective as a neutral but expert foreigner. Shortly after his book was published, there appeared in Spain the so-called critical edition of *The Mystical City of God*, based on Sor María's autograph manuscript and offering a comprehensive introduction. It was competently carried out by a team of Franciscan scholars headed by Father Celestino Solaguren, whose introduction shows a clear will to bring Agredan studies into the second half of the twentieth century. Reflecting his intellectual honesty, as well as a belief in the goodwill and openness of his readers, Solaguren gets into thorny but basic issues that here, too, will be considered. Given the unmistakable strength of Sor María's personality, to what extent is her portrait of the Virgin modeled on herself? To what in her life should be attributed her strong sense of God's immense power and the marvel of his infinitely varied creation? And if, contrary to Franciscan tradition, we are not dealing with the autobiography of the Virgin Mary as told to Sor María de Agreda, what is the literary genre of the work, and what are its sources? I have sought to point the way toward an appreciation of Sor María's writings *a lo humano*, looking at her personality and what it created as neither untouchable icon nor the bizarre outcome of an environment overfull of religious pressures. As Electa Arenal and Stacey Schlau have pointed out, the fundamental value of such nuns' writings is that "these texts contain almost the only record we have of the consciousness of early modern women in Hispanic lands."[13]

Indeed, readers familiar with the panoramic, pioneering studies of Hispanic convent literature by Arenal, which have recently opened up forgotten vistas of a women's literature that a male intellectual tradition had belittled and ridiculed nearly into oblivion, will find in Sor María's writings and life many familiar themes. The cloister, for all its enclosure and the presence of authoritarian confessors, did offer the support of a community of women and a measure of solitude and independence.[14] While Sor María did not become a nun through her own initiative—the decision being her mother's—still, it was the conditions of her life in the convent that gave scope to her administrative talents, stimulated her visions and lent them authority, and called for their recording on paper. An expert seamstress like the Virgin in *The Mystical City of God*, Sor María's position as a gifted nun, like that of her famous Mexican counterpart Sor Juana Inés de la Cruz, gave her the "right to wield not only the needle but the pen."[15] And in their writing, both Sor María and Sor Juana display the curious mixture of exaggerated self-effacement and self-importance that reflects the contradictory demands of patriarchal paranoia and the feminine need to survive with self-esteem.[16]

Close parallels will come to light with the theological feminism of Sor Juana that Arenal has pointed to, notably the Mexican nun's placement of the Virgin "sometimes above, sometimes next to God. . . . Thus she revised patriarchal concepts."[17] Both Sor María and Sor Juana turned to the Virgin as the "Queen of Wisdom," in the Mexican's phrase, Sor María portraying her as a celestial queen as omniscient as her divine spouse and father, and both affirm their worth by establishing comparisons between themselves and heroic figures out of biblical narrative.[18]

The present study publishes for the first time two more Agredan writings and explores their connections to Sor María's presence in the Southwest and to *The Mystical City of God*, both in terms of the ideas themselves and of their place in the trajectory of her writings. They

are, first, *Face of the Earth and Map of the Spheres*, a Renaissance cosmographic treatise presented as a mystical trip around the world and
up into the heavens, but with emphasis on the New World, and second,
the first half of her report to Father Manero, a long letter to the minister general of the Franciscan order in Spain with Sor María's later re-
flections on the bilocation.

Chapters 2 and 3 seek to identify the historic and social forces behind
Sor María's early venture into science, asking to what extent her drive
to know is explained by the Renaissance and by her Jewish ancestry.
Chapter 4 tells of the beginning of her spiritual presence in the New
World, as it was explained not only by the Franciscans, but by Sor
María herself in a quite conventional, rationalistic mode of discourse.
The bilocation serves as a bridge to her more fully imaginative writ-
ings, since while the origin of this incident would appear to be in the
realm of the fantastic, I have considered both the biographical and social factors responsible for it as well as its place in the development of
Sor María's imagination. Chapters 5 and 6 offer an analysis of her imaginative and mystical literary writings, including *The Mystical City of
God*, using the findings of comparative religion in an effort to clarify
not only the reasons for Sor María's literary success, but also the nature
of her symbolic images.

Recent biographies of Sor María in English are no longer in short
supply. Kendrick's is the standard scholarly work, while James Carrico
has a briefer one with a strong Franciscan, hagiographic flavor. Sor
María's legend appears with some prominence in histories of colonial
New Mexico. John Kessell's historical essay on the bilocation is the
most recent, balanced, and thorough look at the circumstances surrounding the origin of Sor María's impact on the Southwest. This study,
which is not intended as another biography, goes into her life only
when it sheds light on her writings. Just a handful of facts are needed
here to suggest the challenging conditions under which Sor María
made a satisfying life for herself and a lasting contribution to the self-
image of women in Hispanic society. In the discussions of the biographical contexts of the writing of each of her works, there is a closer
focus on the texture of her day-to-day living.

Sor María was born into the world of Cervantes, Calderón de la

Barca, Ignacio de Loyola, the Spanish missionary effort to the Americas, San Juan de la Cruz, and, above all, the soon-to-be-canonized Teresa de Avila. Before becoming a nun, her name was María Coronel y Arana, and her parents were exceptionally devout and regularly practiced demanding spiritual, ascetic exercises with the discipline of athletes. As the result of a dream vision experienced the same night by Sor María's mother and her confessor, the family house was converted into a Franciscan convent for women, and the entire family—father, mother, sons, and daughters—joined the order. Although from the time she was a young girl Sor María had been attracted strongly to life as a nun, she suffered intensely, both emotionally and from bad health, during the first three years after taking the vows at seventeen. It is during this period, and perhaps for some years more, that she made repeated mystical journeys to New Mexico, Arizona, and Texas while undergoing trances in Agreda. Although she wanted to keep these events private, her mother, the other nuns in the convent, and her confessor enthusiastically spread the news, and after some years the astonishing story reached the New World, where, according to an official Franciscan report, the Indians themselves confirmed it. She was interviewed on the subject by a Franciscan superior—the same one, in fact, who had first broached the matter with the Indians in New Mexico and then written a celebrated report to the king—and she became quite famous.

While still young, so young as to require a papal dispensation, Sor María was appointed abbess, a post she held for the rest of her life. Energetic in practical as well as religious matters, she was a good fund-raiser and a regular correspondent with influential people in both ecclesiastic and lay circles. Uncompromising in denying the body to enrich the life of the spirit, she slept little and wrote much. But in recording her inner life, Sor María was always under the direction of confessors, one of whom, opposed on principle to women being writers, appears to have been the reason she burned *The Mystical City of God*. (After he died, another commanded her to write it all again.) In 1643, near the midpoint of Sor María's life, Felipe IV, knowing of her through the fame of the Southwestern bilocation, turned aside from his route to the front in the war with France to visit her. A deep and lasting friendship was formed, sustained through frequent letters for thirty years. Following her death and the publication five years later of *The Mystical City*, the church bestowed on her the title of "venerable."

In English history, there is no woman mystic with a comparable political profile, but if we go back some 250 years prior to Sor María's life, well before the English Reformation, we do find parallels in religious life. The most celebrated are Julian of Norwich and Margery Kempe. Kempe, in particular, had much in common with the Counter-Reformation nun. She composed and dictated a book of her own, which though generally considered the first autobiography written in English includes the content of frequent visions. Sor María's life of the Virgin, full of conversations with the protagonist as well as connections to her own life, falls within the same genre of biography fused with introspection. Reminiscent of *The Mystical City of God*, Christ and the Virgin engage Kempe in intimate conversation and instruct her in holy mysteries. And like Sor María's mother, Kempe, believing she was following celestial guidance, convinced her husband, with whom she had lived and raised their children for many years, to abjure forever his marital relations with her. Indeed, both were exceedingly concerned about their sexual purity, and in Kempe's case and that of Sor María and her mother, it is clear that their worry originated both in ecclesiastical teachings about abstinence as a woman's highest form of virtue and in a desire for independence from male control in daily life. Both Kempe and Sor María saw groups of angels attending on them continuously to provide emotional support.

Sue Ellen Holbrook has described Kempe's visions as "mystical, radical, physical and public," which is also an appropriate characterization of Sor María's life of the imagination.[19] It was precisely the radically physical and public nature of the bilocation to North America, as perceived by both enthusiastic Franciscan missionaries and the Inquisitors who investigated the sensational claims made on her behalf, that gained for her at an early age both fame and the king's friendship. And just as Sor María spoke as the voice of conscience in her letters to the king, so, too, Kempe interviewed bishops and spoke with a critical candor that only her manifest aura of saintliness made permissible.

Both Kempe and Sor María practiced severe ascetic exercises and had a keen interest in world travel, the former making pilgrimages that included the Holy Land, while the latter traveled imaginatively.[20] The long trips made by the Virgin in *The Mystical City* similarly seem to reflect a keen desire to be outward bound, leaving the restrictions of a woman's daily round to undertake important missions. Kempe describes other aspects of her spiritual life that also find an echo in the idealized life of the Virgin presented by Sor María: Both are the brides of God at elaborate weddings, both act as God's mother as well as wife, and both participate with extraordinary vicarious intensity in Christ's sufferings on the cross. These similarities between the two women and their visions of the Virgin will be touched on in more detail as the evolution of Sor María's writings is traced.

But if Kempe's book shows that Sor María lived within a cultural tradition not as foreign to the English worldview as most of us had thought, we must return to Spain, and specifically to Teresa de Avila, to see how much the Spanish nun was shaped by and how well she expressed the circumstances of women living within Counter-Reformation Catholicism. The parallels between the two are certainly no coincidence. One reason is that the famous saint from central Spain, the country's co-patroness in Heaven along with Saint James the Greater, not only was revered immensely but was widely read and consciously imitated by Hispanic nuns. As Arenal and Schlau have demonstrated, "Saint Teresa of Avila's impact on the lives and writing of Hispanic nuns can scarcely be overestimated."[21] There were, indeed, many Teresas in the years following her canonization, women who found inspiration in her example to take seriously their visions and their voices. Her positive effects as a role model would be in themselves sufficient demonstration of the importance of the feminist revision of the canon now in progress.

It was repeated often in Agreda that Teresa de Avila had prophesied that the town would produce a most fragrant flower for the garden of the Lord, in effect calling for a future woman to follow in her way. Another, much less well known reason for their parallel casts of mind and resultant actions is that Teresa de Avila and Sor María came from similar families and, therefore, social and religious places in a Spanish society whose heterogeneity was greater than Spaniards have been willing to admit until recently. This factor is explored in chapter 2 in relation to the piece of writing most connected to Sor María's childhood, her *Face of the Earth*.

For an initial illustration of the ties between the two women, we can turn to a kind of writing Sor María did over much of her life, the one part of her work that has been analyzed several times by academic writers: her extensive correspondence with the king. It also shows her abilities in the world of politics and how she related to those in power. Similarly, Teresa de Avila's skills as a letter writer, her strategies for appealing effectively to her readers, have been explicated recently in Alison Weber's study, *Teresa of Avila and the Rhetoric of Femininity*. As a militant reformer within the Discalced Carmelite order, Teresa de Avila was obliged to find ways of persuasion effective with both her followers and the men above her in the ecclesiastical hierarchy. Out of necessity from her position as a woman seeking to exercise power over her own life, and the lives of those in sympathy with her reforms, she developed what Weber has called "the pragmatics of writing as a woman in Counter-Reformation Spain."[22] The guiding principle of that pragmatism was to write what she insisted on saying, but in a style unlike the masculine discourse associated with social power, to write as women were thought to write and so avoid rivalry. Her use of "such 'feminine' features as diminutives, self-depreciation, and self-irony . . . might be better understood as covert strategies of empowerment."[23]

When Felipe IV went out of his way to meet Sor María, she was already forty and an important woman, as Joaquín Pérez Villanueva stresses in his close analysis of their correspondence. The balance of dominance and deference that becomes apparent in their long exchange of thoughts and feelings is not what one might expect, and shows that they both considered her his moral superior and his intellectual equal, although she was also his close friend, with whom he shared his anxieties and joys on a week-to-week basis.

Felipe IV also shared with her and took seriously her ideas on the most challenging parts of his kingly role: politics, war, and finances. For this reason, she has been called, with some exaggeration, the brains of his administration, although it must be pointed out that the unfavorable judgment of history on his effectiveness as a ruler makes the compliment less impressive. Still, she had his confidence and was an undeniable force in his thinking and decision making.

No sycophant, Sor María spoke out sharply against the corruption that was undermining the Spanish court in the twilight of the Spanish Hapsburgs: "Everyone deceives the king. Lord, this monarchy is coming to an end and everyone who does not try to set this right will burn in hell."[24] She was a forthright proponent of peace over war and opposed policies that would further oppress the poor: "For the sake of peace, to lose is to win. . . . Your Majesty should command your advisors to take pity on the helpless poor and your hardpressed vassals, not laying any new burdens on them or wringing blood and sweat from their brows by depriving them of life's necessities."[25]

In religious matters, Sor María acted not only as confessor, to whom the king lamented his seemingly uncontrollable marital infidelities, but also as the voice that exhorted and encouraged him to mend his ways. In another long exchange of letters with the courtier Don Fernando de Borja and his son Francisco, she described herself as the doctor and Felipe as the patient.[26] At her urging, Felipe IV used his royal power to have the Spanish representative to the Vatican argue for acceptance of the belief in the Immaculate Conception as official doctrine. In return, Sor María used her own, visionary power to bring him words of consolation from beyond the grave, from the mouth of his dead son Baltasar Carlos.

In short, the self-deprecating persona often used by Teresa de Avila was not always as necessary for Sor María. A comparison of Teresa de Avila's self-portrait in *The Dwellings*, whose self-affirmation has been described by Weber as disguised and intentionally obfuscated, to that which Sor María projected onto the Virgin Mary in *The Mystical City of God* shows that Sor María, living half a century later, could speak with greater freedom about feminine equality. True, the self-affirmation was not openly her own and was given to a unique, deified woman, but Sor María's writings draw enough parallels between her celestial model and herself to make it clear that her far-from-passive Virgin was a paradigm the author felt to be anything but inimitable.

2

The Renaissance Cosmos and Its Secrets

To understand Sor María's childhood or, more specifically, how her direction as a writer took shape, we might first turn to an account she wrote of her earliest years. Possibly inspired by Teresa de Avila's or other nuns' accounts of their lives, Sor María began an autobiography near the end of her own life, although she died before she was able to describe events later than early childhood. But as Rosa Rossi insists in her biography of Teresa de Avila, one must take such writings not as a reliable source of data but as the expression of a persona created, usually with unconscious inaccuracy, as an essentially fictional character within the narrative.

That caveat may apply to Sor María's case, so I shall put aside for the present the examination of Sor María's late account of how she felt about herself when very young. However, we now have what is, to our knowledge, the earliest work she wrote, *Face of the Earth and Map of the Spheres*. With that, and with information that historians and Hispanists have put together about Sor María's life and society, we can form a better picture than before of how her personality and writing were shaped.

At first glance, it seems contradictory that the mystical Sor María de Agreda should be the author of *Face of the Earth*, a treatise whose subject matter is thoroughly scientific—geography, meteorology, and astronomy. The position of nuns within Renaissance Spanish science was summarized succinctly in 1979 by the leading Spanish historian of the field, José María López Piñero: "Women in religious orders . . . did not participate in scientific activity."[1] However, since López Piñero's emphatic statement, research in women's studies, now vigorously present in Spain, has found evidence of more intellectual activity in Hispanic convents than was previously recognized (although it is true that Juana Inés de la Cruz's and like-minded nuns' literary brilliance remains in the foreground).

Arenal and Schlau, for instance, have studied the works of two sisters who became nuns, María de San Alberto and Cecilia del Nacimiento, and they conclude that "the lives and writings of these two sisters exemplify humanistic culture as it was transplanted to the monasteries of seventeenth-century Spain and its colonies."[2] The sisters' mother was an intellectual and artist whose abilities were recognized even by Felipe II, and their home often received well-educated visitors, including the king's cosmographer and mathematician.

As mentioned earlier, such learned women were more common among the aristocracy at the height of the Spanish Renaissance, in the early years of the sixteenth century, than before or after. As the Counter-Reformation became entrenched, however, the church's institutional agenda was to discourage, or often forbid, women from writing anything that might be construed as authoritative truth, although as Teresa de Avila's canonization shows, there was sometimes tolerance and even popular veneration for women's views in matters of spirituality and mysticism.[3]

It is possibly out of this reluctance to allow women to address "academic" questions as well as from a recognition of how few nuns were in a position to study scientific questions in a modern way that during the eighteenth-century investigation carried out to determine whether Sor María should be canonized, it was officially decided that the work was not authentically hers. That she did in fact write it, as Kendrick has shown and the present chapter makes even clearer, has much to do with the nature of her response to an intellectual and social milieu with which few people today are familiar.

Sixteenth-Century Geography

To understand and dispel surprise at Sor María's Renaissance piece on the natural world, it is helpful to trace the changing attitudes in Spain about science. The idea most commonly expressed in our own century—as current Spanish historians of science document convincingly but lament impatiently—combines two conflicting ideological positions that are at the heart of the so-called "polemic of Spanish science."[4] Numerous treatments in literature (Galdós' novel *Doña Perfecta* being one of the best known) have stressed the gap separating the two Spains in matters of science: for example, the gap between Galdós' benevolent, progressive engineer, Pepe Rey, and the sinister and reactionary clergyman, Don Inocencio, whose thorough classical education serves no good purpose. Curiously, the demands of the debate have led those most apprehensive of technological and social changes to stress how well things have gone in the past, while those who call for change have projected into the past an intellectual poverty that they condemn in the present.

Until recently, an ironic situation existed in which thinkers bent on social change and concerned about science (precisely the people best able to study its historic role) have accepted and made use of a general ignorance of the scientific excellence in Spain during the Renaissance to strengthen their accusation of backwardness against the society of their own time. In the mind of the distinguished twentieth-century philosopher Ortega y Gassett, as in the minds of the forward-looking and scientifically oriented *renovadores* of the two preceding centuries, there was an urgent need to bring from abroad as much as possible of Europe's depository of advanced knowledge. Spain, which was seen as radically different and disconnected, was portrayed as lacking that tradition.

This point of view is well known, as is its partial justification in the undeniable isolation of seventeenth-century Spain from the intellectual revolution transforming the rest of the continent. But as a general rule, the fact that the sixteenth century had been different was conveniently overlooked, and at times even the most obvious was denied: the existence of the Renaissance in Spain and, above all, its scientific dimension. The factors responsible for the country later falling behind were tacitly supposed to have taken hold before the rise of modern science: the rigidity of the Counter-Reformation that combined the fears of an endangered church with the disillusionment and stagnation of a governing class that gradually failed to impose or retain its own way of life in other nations; a profound economic collapse; the policy of attempting to exclude those of Jewish or Moorish descent (*conversos* and *moriscos*) from a productive social role; and the minimal growth of the middle class.

Contrary, then, to what a well-educated group of Spaniards thought for a long time without looking at the facts, Spain enjoyed flourishing scientific activity during at least the first century following its unification under Fernando and Isabel. In the Middle Ages, the mixing of the Arabic and Jewish cultures, which transmitted and developed much of classical learning, did give the country a different inheritance—a source of progress, naturally—while in the sixteenth century under Charles V, the international contacts and prestige generated by the empire favored the growth of humanism. Geography and cosmography were practiced and developed above all because of their application to navigation, the exploration of the New World, and astrology, and there were many professionals in both disciplines. These are the two fields within Spanish Renaissance science that have been most studied in this century, work facilitated by the relatively large number of books originally published in these disciplines. So many were published, in fact, that the reader who is nonplused by the apparent idiosyncrasies of *Face of the Earth* will be doubly surprised on visiting the National Library in Madrid to encounter a varied and extensive collection of sixteenth-century texts all similar in many ways to Sor María's.

Although the identification of all the geographers and cosmographers—classical, medieval, and Renaissance—who directly or indirectly influenced Sor María would have to be done by a specialist, the tradition to which the work belongs had settled and consolidated with time, and the book's basic conformity to that tradition can be sketched with assurance. As in other branches of knowledge, it was Aristotle who created a model that later would be imitated tirelessly, both in the Arabic world that inherited the school at Alexandria and in medieval and Renaissance Europe. His four books *Of the Heavens*, combined with four others entitled *Meteors*, present the concepts of Greek science of his time regarding cosmography, celestial mechanics, and meteorology, and his writings were available in multiple editions, translations, and commentaries all over Europe in the sixteenth century.

A Spanish scholar who was influenced by Aristotle was Isidoro de Sevilla, who wrote *The Etymologies* and *On the Nature of Things* at the end of the Visigothic period. The encyclopedic *Etymologies*, one of the best-known books of the Spanish Middle Ages, includes geographic information that was used for many world maps, and its anecdotal style recalls the narrative style of Sor María's *Face of the Earth*. In astronomy, Isidoro de Sevilla played a considerable role[5] in the establishment of what, until Copernicus, would become the normative celestial model, and the one Sor María reproduced: ten transparent spheres or "heavens" located concentrically enveloping the earth, one or two of the upper ones "aqueous" (separated from the sea during creation as described in Genesis), and above them all the empyrean, the dwelling of God, angels, and the souls of the blessed. As specific textual parallels confirm, the *Etymologies* was one of the works with which Sor María certainly must have been familiar.

The geography of the era, faithfully following that of classical antiquity, was changing less in response to the discoveries in America than one might imagine.[6] Discoveries simply were integrated into the Ptolemaic world, which was divided into four parts and considered inhabited not only by Europeans, Africans, and Asians, but also by three other human groups, mentioned by Sor María: the Antipodes, the Antoecians, and the Perioecians. Some of the works, aiming at maximum scientific rigor, also calculated the latitude and longitude of all the places mentioned.

Sor María's list of each continent's countries, rivers, and cities in *Face of the Earth* was not the first of its kind. She took the descriptions word for word, sometimes abridging, sometimes adding, from the Castilian translation of a cosmographic text widely used in sixteenth-century European universities: *The Book of Cosmography, which Presents the Description of the World and Its Parts, Illustrated with Clear and Attractive Art Work, Supplemented by the Highly Learned Gemma Frisio*. The German author Peter Bienewitz (known in Latin as Apianus) enjoyed extraordinary prestige, and numerous editions and translations of his work contributed to the continuing acceptance of Ptolemaic perspectives.[7] In 1541, Carlos V made him a Knight of the Empire, accompanying the honor with a lavish gift.

Sor María's *Face of the Earth*, in spite of its reproduction of the geographic data in Apianus, is distinguished by its literary nature and the presence of the author as narrator and participant. Isidoro's anecdotes take on more life as Sor María amplifies them and turns them into actions witnessed and commented on by the traveler herself. Where Apianus merely states the existence of Asiatic cannibals, Sor María details a savage custom in which a moaning boy is roasted by his own people, and she vividly expresses her horror. The episode grows out of the common European belief of the time regarding the lamentable state of human life on other continents, and it recalls, for example, the Barbarous Isle of the first section of Cervantes' *The Trials of Persiles and Sigismunda*. On this isle, a false religion demands the bloody sacrifice of foreigners, whose hearts are ripped from their chests. While probably based on accounts of the Aztecs, Cervantes' image is used, as in Sor María's treatise, to build the religious symbolism of the narrative.

Similarly, the strange and even monstrous human races described in classical Greek histories assume new characteristics and take on a richer life and history, reflecting Sor María's concerns and interests. The question of which peoples in fact existed—and to what extent they differed anatomically and morally from the European human norm—fascinated and disturbed her. In this she was typical of the Age of Discovery, but she also touched on a universal interest and literary theme, as mythology and science fiction make clear.

Catholic tradition recorded the opinion of Saint Augustine, who seems to have felt a little perplexed about the issue: "As a consequence, it shouldn't seem absurd to us that within the human race there should be certain monstrous peoples, for this is the same as the cases in which monstrous individuals exist within a people. Therefore, to conclude this question carefully and with circumspection, I shall say that the things written about some peoples are pure fiction, or that, if they are a reality, they are not human beings, or that, if they are human beings, they descend from Adam."[8] Isidoro, on the other hand, was fully convinced: "Therefore, looking at the human race as a whole, there also exist some peoples which are monstrous beings, such as the giants, cynocefalians, cyclops and more."[9]

In his extensively annotated translation to Pliny's *Natural History*,

Francisco Hernández, protophysician and historian for Felipe II, reveals an enthusiasm for these marvels very much in the style of the chroniclers of the first century of American exploration. His enthusiasm doubtless was linked to the taste for all things extraordinary, which is obvious in the chivalric romances of the era and even in the sensational side of Spanish mysticism. But Hernández, bearer of nascent modern science and akin to one side of Sor María's personality, seeks more rational explanations. In this they both reflect the Counter-Reformation zeal to bridle the cognitive and imaginative expansion of the Renaissance. The same standards led Tasso to invent the concept of the "legitimate marvelous," a basic Cervantine literary device.[10] Sor María, although doubtful about a reference to people with no heads, clearly enjoyed these imagined races with astonishment and delicious horror. On comparing her descriptions with the simpler ones found in Apianus, Isidoro, and Pliny, one can see her visual imagination and storytelling ability, although both are less developed than in the later *Mystical City of God*. Her power to convey in words the world of the imagination moves with the same impulse and direction as other accounts of trips to extravagant locations, including *The Divine Comedy*.

The character that Sor María gives to the exceptional beings of *Face of the Earth* differs little from the intellectual and moral pattern she projected onto indigenous Americans. She did not invent that pattern either; its constituent ideas were already in the writings of contemporary historians of the Indies. The 1575 Castilian translation of Apianus, for example, contains an appendix on America drawn from Francisco López de Gómara's work. Moreover, that summary seems to explain the presence in *Face of the Earth* of a long and otherwise hard-to-explain section about an island supposedly closed to Spanish exploration, "that they call Arctic and Antarctic." Sor María says that it was not Christianized by the apostles because its original inhabitants, perverse creatures, did not migrate there until the year 700, a detail that would support Kendrick's assertion that Sor María drew on the medieval concept of Iceland.

Nevertheless, the names and placement in America are better explained by a passage from Apianus: "I want to say, too, that there are many other islands and lands on the face of the earth, in addition to those we have named. One of which is the land of the Strait of Magellan, which turns toward the East, and judging by what has been seen of it, it is extremely large and set very close to the Antarctic pole. They think that one part of it goes toward the Cape of Good Hope and the other toward the Moluccas. So the great size of the earth is not yet fully known."[11] Even the characteristics Sor María attributes to the inhabitants are similar to the 1575 description, although with a conflation of tribes and an additional dose of classical geography.

Sor María's detailed description reveals her enthusiasm as she imagined a people that brings together all that is most bizarre, bestial, and needing to be civilized. They go around naked, and their appearance is hard to distinguish from that of animals. They walk on four feet, which are like those of a bird. Instead of speaking, they only grunt, and the devil must tempt them by means of gestures. Having no houses, they live in burrows. Among them are animals of unknown name—by every indication American buffalo—and Sor María expresses sadness that the people scarcely know how to tell the difference between their essential human condition and that of the beasts. Conscious in her own life of God's immense power and the importance of the small, weak human creature obeying and propitiating him, Sor María is filled with grief and compassion.

Sixteenth-century Spain went through a soul-searching polemic about the treatment of the conquered Indians, and it had been insisted that they were human beings with souls and rights in spite of their living conditions, often thought similar to those of animals. Catholic Spain's duty was not fundamentally to change those conditions; more important was to allow the native Americans to become aware of their souls and how their savagery offended God. The Franciscans, although clearly motivated by humanitarian concerns as well, were the branch of the church entrusted with this basic mission, and its farthest, most glorious frontier during Sor María's childhood was the Kingdom of New Mexico. It therefore became for her, in the context of her own life, the setting where her devotion or, perhaps, her imagination began the story, one very much hers, of the bilocation. Her urge to know the geography of the whole, freshly discovered globe was a step toward the fulfillment of other desires: to leave home, to take action, and to cross the sea on a heroic personal mission.

Cosmography

Copernicus's astronomical thought, published in the middle of the six-teenth century and not condemned by the Inquisition at Rome until 1616, did have a limited acceptance in Spain at the end of the century. Nevertheless, as in the rest of Europe, the traditional medieval system remained dominant. One of the works that most spread its influence was the *Sphera* by John Holywood, an English astronomer of the thir-teenth century, known in Latin as Sacrobosco, and several translations were done in Spain.[12] Later humanist professors introduced popula-rized manuals unburdened by complex mathematics for readers lack-ing a strong background in science. Among the clergy, as López Piñero points out, "it was usual while young to study subjects belonging to the division of arts—mathematics, cosmography, natural philosophy—in preparation for mature years dedicated to theology."[13]

Even a random glance at such texts quickly confirms their ties to Sor María's cosmography. The celebrated professor Alejo Vanegas (or Ve-negas), for example, published several editions of his *Statement of the Differences among the Books Existing in the Universe*, in which the first part is devoted to the natural sciences. It shows the ubiquitous division of the text into the four continents and then the four elements, each of the latter occupying its own niche in the world, the same or-ganization found in Sor María's treatise. Vanegas explains the same phenomena of the natural world as Sor María does: why, for instance, the sea is salty but springs sweet.[14] He makes use of the same termi-nology for the "elemental and celestial" regions, as does Bartholomé Belentín de la Hera y del Varra in his *Repertory of the Specific World of the Spheres of the Heavens and the Elemental Orbs*, and Pedro de Medina in his *Cosmographical Summa*. Like Medina, Sor María ex-tends to the celestial bodies the application of the principle of the four qualities (moist, dry, hot, cold) derived from the four elements. A good example of these parallels in content and even in tone is Medina's en-thusiastic description of the empyrean in his *Book of the Truth*:

> First you should consider the dwelling of the blessed, which is the em-pyrean heaven, so called for its great light and splendor. This heaven is so large and spacious that measuring its immensity is beyond all numbers and proportions. It is so big that, even though there were in it as many

blessed souls as there are drops of water in the sea, and grains of sand on the earth and leaves of trees and blades of grass in all the world, for all there would be more than ample living room. This heaven, as I have said, is very bright, very resplendent, very luminous and beautiful, and very excellent in so many ways that no understanding is sufficient to imagine it, or any human tongue to explain it.[15]

Because of cosmography's kinship to theology at the time, so apparent in *The Divine Comedy*, it was studied frequently by church scholars. An important Franciscan tradition within the field has even been identified running through Roger Bacon, William of Marseille, Saint Buenaventura, and Duns Scotus (whose ideas on the Immaculate Conception are basic to *The Mystical City of God*).[16] In harmony with Saint Francis's own feelings, several learned friars stressed man's amazement in the face of the beauty and immensity of the Creation. Juan de Toledo, for example, bishop of León in 1672 when he published his voluminous *Cursos Theologicos*, wrote a cosmographical treatise very Agredan in its subjects and style. On the first page are praises of the Lord taken from the Book of Psalms. In a similar if more Aristotelian manner, Vanegas featured the phrase, "the creatures proclaim the first cause, which is God."[17] The importance among Spanish Franciscans of the idea of the world as a book proclaiming the greatness of God was studied by Laura Calvert: "In the early sixteenth century, the Franciscan known as Francisco de Osuna echoed the phrase, giving the 'book of the creatures' an importance almost equal to that of the Bible as a revelation of the Divine. His creatures are not limited to those in Biblical passages. They may come from the sciences—the negative afterimage of sight or the principal of the pump; the arts of ironworking or music—and plants and animals of the world."[18]

This Franciscan perspective, from as early as the work of William of Marseille, had drawn upon the system of Ahmed Mohamed Ibn Kathair al-Fergani, an Arabic cosmographer of the ninth and tenth centuries known in Europe as Alphraganus.[19] Taking the Greek astronomers' texts as his starting point, he arrived at figures not only for the diameters of the sun, the moon, the five planets, and the six magnitudes of stars, but also the "exact" distance to the celestial spheres, a feat of ingenuity and creative geometry that earned him the title of "The Calculator." He stressed the smallness of the earth, suspended motionless like a grain of sand in the center of the immense, rapidly rotating heavens, and to each of the heavens he ascribed a considerable thickness, a distance large enough to allow the planet to move in an epicycle between its apogee and its perigee (i.e., its farthest and closest positions in relation to the earth). There existed, therefore, one distance to the lower or "concave surface," and another, substantially greater, to the upper or "convex surface."

The numbers generated by such calculations, however, varied wildly from astronomer to astronomer when others sought in vain to perfect Alphraganus' methodology over the succeeding centuries. Even the diameter of the earth was not universally agreed upon. The Jesuit father known by the Latin name Clavius, who directed the Gregorian revision of the calendar, includes in his commentary on Sacrobosco a table comparing the calculations of Aristotle, Hiparcus, Erathosthenes, Ptolomeus, Alphraganus, Fernelius, and "more recent astronomical experts."[20] He himself opined that Alphraganus was the closest to the truth.

To get an idea of the variety of results obtained, and the extent to which these terrestrial-planetary, medieval-Renaissance dimensions were bandied about in the scientific world, it is instructive to make some comparisons among cosmographers. The following table lists the distances to the spheres of Mercury and of Saturn as calculated by Alphraganus, Clavius (who takes them from Francisco Maurolico), Vanegas (who says he takes them from Alphraganus, although that's not clear to me, and who also mentions a method by Gemma Frisius), Juan de Toledo (who does seem to be based on Alphraganus), and Sor María de Agreda.

	SPHERE OF MERCURY	SPHERE OF SATURN
Alphraganus[21]	208,545 miles	46,816,250 miles
Clavius[22]	1,443,750 miles	323,512,500 miles
Vanegas[23]	334,209 miles	18,541,250 miles
Juan de Toledo[24]	75,369 leagues	17,154,631 leagues
S. María de Agreda	7,901,917 leagues	8,505,119,514 leagues

It is not at all obvious on which of many contradictory authorities Sor María might have based her calculations. The *vice-postulador* entrusted with the current efforts for her canonization, Father Ruipérez, has suggested that she might have multiplied some preexisting figures by a mystically ascertained constant. What is certain is her unfailing consciousness of the greatness of God and his Creation—here expressed in millions of leagues.

Date and Authenticity of *Face of the Earth*

In spite of so many points of contact with this venerable cosmographic tradition, the question of what Sor María read is not simple. She herself sought to dismiss consideration of sources in evaluations of her work, insisting that her knowledge was the fruit of heavenly inspiration, "infused science," or "infused knowing," and that so much information in an uneducated woman could only be explained in this way. Certain facts, however, suggest that her attitude was in large part a conventional one imposed by her social circumstances as a woman. Aside from the quotations and sources in *Face of the Earth*, Sor María states in her report to Father Manero that she can read Latin and distinguish between good and bad translations from that language. In *The Mystical City of God*, she shores up the authenticity of events with footnotes referring to passages in history books. And one of her confessors, Fray Andrés de Fuenmayor, affirmed that Sor María could talk about geography and cosmography as though she had studied them in school.[25]

Father Solaguren and his collaborators in the recent "critical" edition of *The Mystical City of God*, willing to accept the possibility of human as well as divine sources of inspiration, attempted to trace details of the Virgin's life as told by Sor María by searching in the apocryphal gospels and popular traditions. One of the editors said they could not find details similar to those in Sor María's narrative expansions of the biblical story, although my own inference runs counter to that conclusion. In any case, their position, as illustrated by the encyclopedic nature of *The Mystical City of God*, is not unreasonable: Sor María apparently had an exceptional memory and capacity for synthesis. From the time she was a little girl, friars from the men's convent at Agreda had visited the house, and later she heard their sermons and confessorial advice while living out her life in the women's convent. Although the friars certainly would have lent her books, and the convent has a collection that dates from the earliest years, one may suppose that much of the vast theological and biblical information in her masterpiece was acquired by listening. Still, *Face of the Earth* shows that this oral communication was complemented by reading.

At what point in her life Sor María wrote her cosmographical treatise, a circumstance clearly related to her access to books, is also uncertain. Kendrick (who echoes the positivistic nineteenth-century scholars' view that the little book is just an accumulation of errors and absurdities) considers it a childhood work, written before taking orders, and motivated by a wish to display recently acquired knowledge to impress her two younger brothers. To support this hypothesis, he gives capital importance to Sor María's statement in the prologue that she was writing to inspire love of the Creator in "her brothers." It must be noted, however, that in a prologue written later, Sor María uses the same expression clearly meaning all people, her brothers and sisters in Christ. It was a common expression in the period, especially in Franciscan writings, and one could argue that she used it to achieve the sound of masculine discourse and to gain the societal approval that went with it.

On beginning to write her autobiography at the end of her life, apparently having just reread *Face of the Earth*, Sor María felt again the desire that her work might inspire devotion in everyone, but now the language is more inclusive: "I confess to Heaven and to Earth that, as I look at these events with greater understanding and enlightenment than when I received them, and reflecting on what the Most High has deigned to do, my heart dissolves in loving tenderness, and how I wish that my chest would burst with a voice heard from east to west and from north to south, calling out to all the children of Adam, inviting and begging them to employ all their energies in knowing and serving such a Lord. . . ."[26]

There are, however, other reasons for believing she must have written the book in her youth, in the years just before the bilocation, and that is how her close friend Samaniego, her Franciscan superior and first biographer, presents it. The enthusiasm in *Face of the Earth* for the beauty and variety of Creation, the sensation of flying around the world carried by angels; the desire to help convert the New Mexican Indians—everything points toward Sor María's adolescence and the first, trying years of life in the convent when she felt she was carried across the sea. In her autobiography, Sor María says that twice God had shown her all things created:

> The first time was when I first became capable of rational thought; the second, when through infused knowing I was prepared to write the life of the Queen of Heaven, Most Holy Mary. On the occasion I am describing, I saw things but took in their beauty on the surface, yet still perceiving the Creator in them; I was moved to love and serve Him, and became aware that their being, arrangement, and ordered functioning depended on divine wisdom and power. Great was this kind gift and benefit, second only to knowing God, and with it I suddenly went from ignorance of all things to wisdom about them.[27]

A few paragraphs earlier, Sor María says that after her first contact with supernaturally imparted knowledge of the world, she entered a period of ordinary human perception and learning:

> Since I received the teaching and discipline of divine knowing when as ignorant as I have said, and suddenly so many mysteries were shown to me, giving me the capacity to know and penetrate them, as has been described, when that passive teaching ceased, I came down to the five senses and made good use of them. I was astonished at both what I had learned and at what I was now seeing with my own eyes and outside my own head; and like one who unexpectedly discovers new and precious things and is left amazed, so it happened to me.[28]

Even as a purely human observer of the world as a child, Sor María says she was intellectually precocious because "the understanding with which I knew all that is created was more advanced than my age, for the Most High enlarged my mind's capacity."[29] She underlines the different nature, relative to ordinary learning and to her first mystical experience, of the second supernatural revelation, experienced when she was fully mature: "Greater beyond compare was the second time, because the right hand of the All Powerful infused into my mind knowledge of the universe more abundantly than the first. I came to know the being of all things, their qualities and properties, with great penetration and perception of distinctions, as I shall say at the appropriate moment."[30]

It can be supposed then, without contradicting her own memories, that during her childhood, Sor María probably acquired her cosmographical knowledge through reading and put it down on paper in a first version of *Face of the Earth*. Years later she might easily have modified, amplified, and polished that juvenile draft, perhaps in the enthusiasm of writing *The Mystical City of God*, or even remembering in old age the second cosmographic revelations of her mature years, when she was writing her great narrative. Other circumstances, found in connection with the prologues for the treatise written at the end of her life, suggest this last possibility.

Until a century after Sor María's death, no one suggested that *Face of the Earth* might not be authentic. Several compilations of her writings during those years include it as hers without comment or question, and I had the opportunity to look through the three copies preserved in the collection of Sor María's works at the convent in Agreda. Sor María herself, in the prologue to her autobiography, includes it in the list of her works.[31] Both Father Samaniego and Father Salizanes, who knew her and her handwriting well, were sure of it. Fray Antonio de Jesús, director of the campaign for Sor María's canonization in the last quarter of the seventeenth century, carried out the project of locating and legally certifying valid copies of her writings immediately after her death, and among them is *Face of the Earth*. On more than one manuscript he wrote to the effect that Father Salizanes had the original in Cordoba and had not allowed Samaniego to have more than one copy made.[32] In fact, the convent's archives preserve a letter from Samaniego, dated October 14, 1665, promising to return all the original autograph manuscripts to the nuns. These two friars, superiors and friends of Sor María, accompanied her at the time of her death and two days later locked away all her writings in a "chest with three locks," the inventory of which includes the "books . . . of the perfections of the heavens and the earth."[33] This fact, though not conclusive, weakens Kendrick's hypothesis that one of Sor María's two younger brothers had the original and later handed it over to Salizanes.

In addition to this physical evidence, the ideas and personal traits linking *Face of the Earth* to Sor María's accepted works carry the greatest weight. Aside from the testimony that it offers for her interest in science, the text is creative and of interest primarily as literature. The difficulties with her figures, pointed out by the anonymous author of an arithmetic study appended to the 1724 manuscript under the title "Adjustment and Liquidation of the Heights, Diameters, Semi-diameters of the Terrestrial Globe and the Ten Heavens," remind us that even in its time the work was not considered rigorously scientific. That circumstance, along with the proscriptive and descriptive objections to the combination of nuns and science—not to mention the borrowings from Apianus—must have influenced the theologians of the Congregation of Rites, who in a year as scientifically "enlightened" as 1762, discarded *Face of the Earth* as not authentically by Sor María.[34]

To educated readers, the treatise always has seemed neither fish nor fowl, neither mysticism nor science. Although at first glance *Face of the Earth* seems a natural candidate for mathematical tables of the sort that abound in authors like Father Clavius (an authority cited in the "Adjustment"), the circumferences have been calculated very badly from the diameters, using the number 3 instead of pi. The author of the appendix expresses his bewilderment and can only reassure himself regarding this anomaly by reflecting that Sor María had personally seen and touched the spheres; however, that obviously is not the verifiable type of experiment now considered the hallmark of trustworthy knowledge.

What, then, does this expression of a strong impulse toward Renaissance science have to do with Sor María's more literary, mystical works like *The Mystical City of God* and with the visions that gave rise to the legendary bilocation? In a word: knowledge. From that early moment in her life when in a vision God showed her the whole world, until the mature years when she wrote in *The Mystical City of God* that the same experience was granted to the Virgin, Sor María de Agreda was motivated by an unmistakable desire to participate in the Creator's knowledge.

What is typical of the Renaissance here is, first, Sor María's urge toward encyclopedic knowledge. Witness the survey of all that can be known in a later work that nonetheless still breathes the spirit of the Spanish Renaissance, the *First Dream* by Sor Juana Inés de la Cruz (who included Sor María among the learned women from whom she had drawn inspiration).[35] Second is the typical organization of information in a logical order, clarifying the relations among the many headings and subdivisions. *Face of the Earth* is structured this way, and even more so is *The Mystical City of God,* which recounts the history of the universe from the Creation to the Final Judgment—exactly the recipe that readers of Renaissance literature may recognize; Lope de Vega recommends it in his *New Art of Making Plays* as an effective technique to hold the attention of a Spanish audience. But *The Mystical City* does so with a clearly structured outline, including divisions into books, chapters, and numbered paragraphs. Unlike Teresa de Avila, Sor María did not make strategical use of the stereotypically disordered, illogical "prattle" that Counter-Reformation Spain attributed to women.[36] Just as she dared to converse on equal footing with her good friend the king, so too she dared to express her undeniably self-asserting ideas in the approved style of masculine discourse.

The final chapter, on *The Mystical City of God,* traces the importance in Sor María's work, from her earliest years as we know them in the autobiography, of the connection between acquiring knowledge and access to some measure of power—between, in broader terms, knowing and emotional security. The evolution of Western ideas reminds us that the Renaissance stressed the same connection, and that the roots of modern science are in alchemy and magic. As the legend of Doctor Faustus dramatizes, the scientific quest flows from an urge to enlarge the possibilities at the command of the individual, who seeks to enhance her own potential by uncovering powerful knowledge unknown to others.

This drive is certainly tied to the other Renaissance phenomenon represented by Sor María: Spanish mysticism. I would be quick to add, however, that it developed without an option for an openly rebellious personal ambition like that expressed in pronounced literary form by writers such as Marlowe and Goethe. Among Spanish mystics, the enforced traditions of Christian humility and monastic obedience almost always controlled Luciferic pride, and the Inquisition took care to extirpate the more rebellious of the charismatic *alumbrados.* Nonetheless, Teresa de Avila and, to a considerable extent, Sor María were convinced that they were specially called to change the world, and they energetically tried to do so through both their writing and political activities in spite of the Inquisition's paternal frown.

In principle, then, there is nothing inexplicable in Sor María's thirst for knowledge, combining book knowledge (which in the Renaissance had come to include personal observations and experiments as supplementing the authority of writers hallowed by the centuries) with an "infused science" based on personal experiences flowing from the highest authorities in the Christian tradition—voices from Heaven and the Creator himself. Francisco Márquez Villanueva has argued that sixteenth-century Spain offered an alternative approach to the Modern Age, one that did not oblige it to break with the medieval theocentric world view.[37] He points to this same mixture of science and mysticism, a dual mode of knowing, in several figures from the period. For example, Juan de Avila was a contemplative and also an avid experimenter, notably with hydraulic systems.[38] Luis de León took inspiration from the beauty of the perfect regularity of the stars' movement across the sky, and Vanegas juxtaposed books based on human reason with those written through divine revelation. Sor María, for her part, took a standard college text as the point of departure and supplemented it with the description of a mystical "flight" that could supply new "data" not found in her traditional, bookish source. As Catherine Swietlicki has pointed out, Jewish mysticism was appropriated eagerly by many Renaissance scholars drawn to alchemy and magic. Cabala's promise to grant access to God's secret powers appealed to "humanism's fascination with the esoteric."[39]

But Vanegas, Juan de Avila, and Luis de León did not mix cosmographical geography and arithmetic with data intuitively received from Heaven. And as we have seen, women in religious orders—for whom research was not thought appropriate—rarely participated in science. What, then, explains Sor María's mystically scientific writing? Part of the answer may lie in Sor María's, and Teresa de Avila's, Jewish descent.

The Converso Legacy

Various explanations have been offered for the remarkable flowering of charismatic spirituality in sixteenth- and seventeenth-century Spain. In reviewing the sources of *iluminismo*, Mary Giles has pointed out parallels in several religious traditions—Islam, German mysticism, Judaism, Erasmianism, Lutheranism, Anabaptism, and medieval Christian heresies—though at its root there was, she concludes, a "desire to nurture an inner life of prayer that, for the most part, was an integral part of Catholic practice."[40]

In tracing the ecclesiastical currents that led to the later prominence of Teresa de Avila, Weber focused on the first half of the sixteenth century in Spain as a period in harmony with, although it arose independently from, the spirit of the Protestant Reformation.[41] Before the misogynistic Counter-Reformation moved to discredit a growing importance for women's spiritual gifts within the church, Cardinal Ximénez Cisneros encouraged the inner life of prayer, gave women a larger role to play in administering convents, and defended women visionaries. Thus Teresa de Avila encountered changing and mixed cultural attitudes, with much gained in society at large but then discouraged by the church hierarchy during the second half of her life. Sor María's life and writings confirm the idea that in the broadest historical context, both the Renaissance and the religious upheaval of the Reformation were about individuals taking knowledge, power, and inner peace into their own hands. Even Kempe in the late Middle Ages received a similar vision: Christ, while not speaking ill of church ceremonies, made her understand that they could not provide as much intimacy between him and the soul as was to be desired.[42]

Religious enthusiasm, as seen in the mystical nature of Saint Francis's belief in union with God through an intensely emotional experience related to human love, certainly was transmitted to Spain as a part of orthodoxy through mystics like Catherine of Siena. Less clear are the circumstances within Renaissance Spain that led to the exceptional development and widespread acceptance of that tradition as a desirable way of life. One explanation has been developed by literary critics like Swietlicki, who have argued for the decisive influence of Jewish and Muslim culture during the Middle Ages and the Renaissance.

In this context, the special intensity of mysticism in sixteenth-century Spain is best understood in relation to the high percentage of conversos who, whether or not they took religious orders in a faith not of their ancestors, became either *alumbrados*, rejected by the church, or orthodox mystics. During the Middle Ages, two sharply contrasting tendencies coexisted within the Spanish Jewish population. One was philosophical and rational, harboring a substantial element of skepticism and a view of God that T. A. Perry has called medieval Jewish existentialism.[43] The other tendency, in which God, his power, and purposes were more accessible, was emotional and mystic. Both views were cultivated through an active writing of books as different as those of the cabala and those in the tradition of the rational philosopher-physician Maimonides. The role of Spanish Jews as translators and transmitters of Greek-Arabic science and philosophy for a Latin-reading Europe reinforced Jewish preeminence in the learned professions and gave extra vigor to a Jewish way of life based on books.

Even after and notwithstanding the forced baptisms of the fifteenth century, conversos continued to be influential both intellectually and socially although they were resented for it, as suggested by the creation of discriminatory "clean blood" statutes by competing groups. According to López Piñero, "Jewish conversos were the most important demographic base for scientific activity," even though some "developed their scientific activity while straddling exile and Spanish society. . . . Luis Núñez Coronel, also from Segovia, accomplished a notable contribution to physics from his chair at the College de Montaigu in nominalist Paris without for that reason disconnecting himself from Castile."[44]

Those who subscribed to the rationalist and skeptical current within Hispano-Jewish thought reacted to the loss of social rights with desperation, bitterness, and irony, creating works like Fernando de Rojas' *Celestina* and contributing heavily to the whole genre of the picaresque. The mystic tendency, in marked contrast, led to a fervent embrace of Catholicism, producing inquisitors and members of religious orders who did everything possible to show the purity of their faith, if not that of their blood, through heroic devotion and extraordinary zeal. They also passed on their mystical inheritance, a circumstance that not coincidentally allowed a converso writer like Teresa de Avila to appeal her grievances and sorrows directly to the bar of divine justice. That legacy naturally influenced the nature of mystical life. Writing about Luis de León in 1988, Joseph Silverman commented that his "'mysticism' derives from a mixture of poetry and philosophy, reminiscent of the Cabalistic poetic tradition, and founded on a passionately intellectual curiosity about the origins of life and an unswerving contemplative devotion to God and His creations."[45]

Doubters have argued about how many generations of "new Christians" would keep alive their parents' worldview, but social discrimination throughout the sixteenth and seventeenth centuries, combined with the Jewish culture's usual resolute persistence in the face of adversity, seems to make the four or five generations of the sixteenth century not an improbably long time. Swietlicki, like Stephen Gilman a generation earlier, has shown the degree to which Jewish culture was alive and integrated into Spanish life in Sor María's lifetime: "Cabala was an integral part of the popular culture and folk customs to which [Santa Teresa] was heir, as a descendant of conversos and as a member of Spanish society."[46]

Evidence of Sor María's Jewish descent is her father's family name of Coronel, a prominent name that invariably went back to Fernando and Isabel's chief tax collector, who converted in 1492. Because an important character in Quevedo's picaresque novel *El buscón* is named Diego Coronel, the name has been researched thoroughly. Luis F. Peñalosa and Carroll B. Johnson have shown with abundant sources that the several branches of the Coronels, all derived from a common source, were characterized by scholars and politicians.[47] Although important throughout Castile, the Coronels were centered in Segovia, where in the sixteenth century one neighborhood bore their name. That neighborhood's location in the Jewish quarter was the circumstance that first alerted modern researchers to the name's origin.[48]

Pérez Villanueva has brought together similar facts about the conversos and, specifically, about Sor María's family name of Coronel:

> Caro Baroja . . . supplies information about the Coronels being conversos. Abraham Senior, of Segovia, converts and takes the name of Fernán Pérez Coronel. A. Domínguez Ortiz . . . studied this figure, who was the head of the converso lineage of the Coronels. The granddaughter of Senior was María Coronel, wife of the participant in the Comunero revolt Juan Bravo. . . . Sometimes—according to Caro—conversos would take old lineages that had almost disappeared. . . . Juan of Vallejo, in his famous Memorial . . . refers to a professor Coronel who took part in the editing of the Polyglot Bible and was a "townsman from Alcalá, a Catholic Christian, a convert from Judaism and very learned in the Hebrew and Chaldean languages.[49]

Sor María's parents were extraordinarily devout, engaged in bodily exercises of self-mortification and, moreover, seeing supernatural interventions in their lives. Such manifestations of religious fervor often grew from the social circumstances that so strongly bounded the lives of conversos, for they lent a highly visible intensity (and guarantee for society) to the sincerity of the new faith. The custom would have started two or three generations before Sor María's parents, when a desire to wash out what some considered the fresh stain of Judaism would have called religious fervor into existence. But the way of life would have been passed down to children and grandchildren even when its origins might have been hidden successfully and even forgotten. What is more, there is specific evidence that the Jewish mystical tradition reached Sor María de Agreda, as it had reached Teresa de Avila, in the form of Christian cabala. Sor María's treatise on the six angels who attended to her mixes a surprising amount of cabalistic imagery and concepts with Christian angelology.[50]

The parallels between Sor María's and Teresa de Avila's family situations are revealing. Both grew up in small towns in Old Castile with populations of about 100, in large stone houses that still can be visited today, houses that testify to an above-average social position.[51] However, both fathers struggled, like many *hidalgos* at the time, against a declining level of income, and though married to women from old Christian families, both were four or five generations removed from wealthy Jewish ancestors who had converted to Christianity. In Teresa de Avila's case, it had been her great-grandfather, whose son had moved to Avila from Toledo after being publicly punished for lapsing into Judaism. Rossi argues that Teresa de Avila must have known about the carefully guarded secret of her Jewish descent, though she left no reference to it. It is harder to know about Sor María. The cabalistic content of her *Six Angels* suggests that she did know of her Jewish ancestry, but Swietlicki has pointed out that cabalistic ideas were adopted by many Christian writers in the Renaissance, and Spanish society had incorporated many Jewish traditions into what was thought of as purely Christian.

Teresa de Avila's father's social strategy for coping with his Jewish ancestry was, in Rossi's words, "to appear to others as an hidalgo even though he knew he was not one."[52] A lavish lifestyle, which he could not afford, and the creation of disastrous debts were the result. Sor María's father, who was given to exaggerated displays of painful, penitential piety, might well be viewed as following a parallel pattern in the sphere of religion. Whether his generation of the family knew of their ancestry or whether he simply inherited a way of life, the loss of his house and lands for a convent represents a similar economic denouement to the same story of radical insecurity. This pattern also includes the fact that Sor María's and Teresa de Avila's childhoods came to an end as they became nuns under pressure from their families, who required the girls to acquiesce to meet the families' needs. Writing about Teresa de Avila's converso family background in connection with becoming a nun, Arenal and Schlau observe that "for her, as for other women whose Christianity was in doubt, the cloister afforded better protection from accusations than did the secular world."[53] And while Kempe was not of Jewish descent, Susan Dickman has pointed out that whatever its inward function, her frequent, seemingly uncontrollable sobbing in public when she was moved by compassion for Christ's suffering was useful as a demonstration of her piety, a piety that her life in the world instead of the cloister seemed to call into question.[54]

This is not to say there were no other reasons for women to enter convents. Sor Juana Inés de la Cruz is a famous example of someone who chose to enter a convent in the interest of pursuing the life of the mind. Another powerful consideration was freedom from masculine control over one's body, whether from domestic violence, or the dangers of repeated pregnancy and childbirth, or the lack of opportunity to live the church's ideal of holy celibacy. Still, Teresa de Avila's and Sor María's full and joyful acceptance of the decision to enter a life thought of as apart from the world appears to have come sometime later. Similarly, the young Kempe longed to be favorably noticed and turned to an intensely spiritual life only after failing in the milling and brewery businesses, which she entered in an effort to earn money for fine clothes.

Little is known about Sor María's education, although *Face of the Earth* shows that she read textbooks, even incorporating one into a fantasy of leaving home and being taken around the world. Since, in Spain, traditional Jewish respect for books fused with the Renaissance quest for knowledge, a studious girl might well have been a conversa, but not necessarily. In the early sixteenth century, before the rejection of Erasmian reform calling for education of women, wealthy Spanish families often provided their daughters with tutors and home study, sometimes advanced. A century before Sor María's childhood, Isabel la Católica hired Italian humanists to teach her two daughters, one of whom, Catalina, the first wife of Henry VIII of England, was considered amazingly learned by Erasmus and Sir Thomas More.[55]

Teresa de Avila, though not learned, avidly read saints' lives and chivalric romances and tried to live the heroics they describe, including an unsuccessful attempt to run away from home with her brother so they might reach pagan lands and be beheaded for the faith. They also wrote a romance of love and adventure, which probably provided the same sort of emotional outlet represented by Sor María's writing of her horror and compassion as angels showed her the strange customs of peoples around the world.

In sum, both Sor María and Teresa de Avila, with a focus on books typical of conversos, nurtured ideas of their place in the world through them. Also, both families had a history of turning to religion for social authentication. In light of growing knowledge about the circumstances of conversos in seventeenth-century Spain, and the Jewish origins of the Coronel family, one can conclude that the combination of science and mysticism in Sor María's work did not arise only from the influence of the Spanish Renaissance. It also arose from the fusing of two ways of life, one broadly scientific and the other mystical; both were traditional in the influential converso sector of Spanish society but already for more than a century adapted and reshaped in a continuing attempt at cultural and personal survival. In Sor María's writings, one can see a parallel to the response of Spanish intellectuals of Jewish descent to their adverse fortunes in the period, similar to her own search for happiness under very restricted circumstances as a woman who never left Agreda.

From the perspective of sociological interpretation, then, the historical and family factors in the human formula behind the success of Sor María's famous book would be the mind as power in human relations, clarity and organization of information, and intense emotional commitment to uncovering, through either experimental or mystical "knowing," the secrets permitting salvation of difficult lives, salvaging happiness in both the inner and social worlds.

Manuscripts of *Face of the Earth*

The location of Sor María's autograph manuscript is unknown; there has been no trace of it since Salizanes had it at the Cathedral of Cordoba. Aside from the three copies at the convent in Agreda (with no indication of their connection to the original), there are ten in the National Library, identified by Serrano y Sanz.[56] Conversations with archivists familiar with Spanish Franciscan writings confirm my impression that *Face of the Earth* was widely known and copied in manuscript form; its mystical theme and the protracted Vatican investigation of *The Mystical City of God* would explain why it was never printed in spite of a substantial demand by readers. Brief published descriptions of copies of *Face of the Earth* include one from the Public Library of Toledo.[57] Agueda Jiménez has been kind enough to give me a photocopy of one preserved at the Public Library of Guadalajara, Mexico. The large number and uneven quality of the manuscript copies of all of Sor María's works is explained well by Angel Uribe:

> The fame of her writings flies from mouth to mouth and her admirers felt a common desire to obtain copies and refresh their spirit with reading them. To satisfy this urge numerous copies hurriedly made were distributed, and these were not always of reliable accuracy, either because the scribes were inadequately trained, or because on occasion surreptitious copies were made under time pressures that limited comparison with the original, or because the copies taken as the model were deficient, or because, as a way to extricate themselves from other difficulties, some copyists attributed to the mystic writer and placed under the mantle of her protective authority texts fathered by someone else. For all these reasons it is no surprise today to find in both official and convent libraries in any corner of Spain manuscript copies of works by the Venerable Mother.[58]

The present edition is based on a manuscript preserved in the Royal Library of El Escorial and described in the catalogue written by Julián

Zarco Cuevas.[59] Evidence for its early date include the handwriting (from the middle of the seventeenth century according to Zarco Cuevas) and a colloquial and spontaneous style that contrasts sharply with the eighteenth-century versions, which are more polished and stylistically corrected. It is also one of the copies legalized by Antonio de Jesús. Moreover, on the first three folios of the volume that contains it, there appears the following note, evidently added later by a friar resident in El Escorial, on the origins and authenticity of the writings found therein:

> This volume, along with two others of the same size though somewhat thicker, have for more than eighty years been passed together from hand to hand among the friars of this monastery, it being a tradition among them that they belonged to the distinguished Señor Don fray Antonio Agustín, illustrious son of our monastery of Santa Engracia and former bishop of Alvarracín from the year 1665 to that of 1670, in which he died.
>
> This tradition is based on the word of the first person who brought them into the house, who was Father fray Joseph del Valle, known also as the Benedictine father, and who assisted His Excellence throughout the latter's entire episcopate and later lived here highly regarded until the year 1692. On his death they were given to Father fray Juan de Aguirre, a great servant of God, who died on August 3, 1727; from him they went to another friar who is still alive and who after a few years handed them over to Father fray Antonio de San Joseph, the senior librarian, so that the latter, if he thought fit, might place them in the library among the manuscripts. But since the said Father fray Antonio died on March 24, 1732, without having done so—nor does the reason for that happen to be known—they were returned to the possession of the friar who had given them to him, and he decided, lest they be misplaced or lost, to return them to the library in case they might be useful in the future.
>
> The first volume, which is all works by the Venerable Mother Superior de Jesús de Agreda, contains four treatises. The first is the laws that the Lord intimated and made known to his wife so that she might be perfect. The second, the discipline of divine knowing. The third, part of *The Mystical City of God* that this venerable mother superior wrote, and it goes through the end of chapter fifteen, which is halfway through the infancy of Our Lady in the temple. But it is somewhat different from the one that is circulating in print, so it may be part of what the said venerable

mother superior originally wrote in the year 1637. And the fourth is a daily exercise to spend the day well, and it fills half or more of the volume.

The second volume, which is likewise by the same venerable mother superior under the same title of Laws for the Wife, contains at the beginning the two first treatises of the first volume with very slight differences, but then adding different doctrines and other things that Our Lady taught her. And after this, as a separate work, a treatise on the infused knowledge that her soul received about the face of the earth, its inhabitants, etc., and about the elements and the heavenly region.

Now since someone might possibly doubt that these writings are by the said mother superior—in the first place because it is true that in the year 1645 she burned all her works at the instructions of one of her confessors, second because none of them has to date appeared in print among the others of hers that are in circulation, and finally because in these writings one finds some imperfections unbecoming a distinguished person like Señor Don fray Agustín, all of which would seem to dissuade one from believing that his excellence had them—but I feel that although these facts that have been brought forward are true, still it is also true that the venerable mother superior wrote all the treatises contained in the said two books, as is stated by the Most Reverend Father fray Joseph Ximénez Samaniego in several places in the biography that he wrote and which is published in the first volume of *The Mystical City of God* (especially in paragraphs 12, 21, 22, and 25), and also that a very respectable member of his order who had a special devotion for the venerable mother superior made a copy for himself, although with the flaws to be expected when done surreptitiously, of many of her early works and kept them until his death (these are the very words of the said most reverend father in paragraph 22[60] and in the "Defense and Prologue," paragraph 12); and above all since it is certainly true that His Excellence, before becoming bishop, was in very close communication with the venerable woman, as is demonstrated by eighteen letters of hers that are found in this library of San Lorenzo (which doubtless were also brought here along with the books by the same friar), so that it seems to me not only not unlikely, but on the contrary very probable, that either through his own initiative or as a gift someone might have wanted to give him that these books came into his possession, and that having naturally formed a high opinion of the venerable mother superior's virtues and holiness through the correspondence just mentioned he would have highly valued them and kept them until his death. Finally, we say just what we know and we offer what we are able, without trying to pressure anyone to change his views or to lend more authority to the manuscripts than they deserve. But it seems to us they are not contemptible simply because they are naive.

The third volume contains various accounts of some extraordinary events and other things related to a servant of God called Isabel Trilles, known also as Isabel de Jesús María, who seems to have flowered in Valencia as a lay person at the same time as María de Agreda, especially from the year of 1661 to that of 1666, and these things were written down as they were happening by her confessor, Father Ginés Berenguer of the Company of Jesus, as is recorded and can be seen several places in the same volume, which is very naive and not even written in the best form, as anyone will be able to observe. For this reason and in order to learn what authority and truth could be attributed to this piece, not having been able to find anything on the subject in our library, a letter was sent to Madrid to Don Joseph Tormo, a Valencian and Doctor of Theology, who replied that according to what he had heard and gathered from others from that region, the Venerable Trilles flowered in Valencia as a lay person highly reputed for her virtues, a reputation she kept through the end of her life, and whose good qualities were preached about; in Valencia, Father Ginés Berenguer, her confessor, has her life written down, and in the biography he has said wonderful things about her lofty holiness. These are the very words from the letter of the said doctor, and they agree very well with what is stated in the said treatise. And so I feel that in spite of the substantial defects that are obvious in it, one may with good conscience keep it for whatever value it may have in the future.

I have designated this manuscript "A," for Fray Antonio Agustín. Unfortunately, it lacks the prologue, and the map itself is incomplete, going only as far as the section on the first heaven. Curiously, the same is true for the legalized copy preserved in the National Library, and I have been obliged to make use of another seventeenth-century copy, one apparently reliable but lacking any data about its filiation. I refer to it as "K," from its old call number (KK, papeles curiosos, 15). It must be asked whether the treatise is hers only up to the point where, in some manuscripts, it breaks off unfinished. This is certainly a logical possibility and one strengthened by the diminishing of her personal voice and the predominance of pure numbers after that point. Nevertheless, the preambles to the work and the title itself of *Map of the Spheres*, in the plural, weaken the argument, for it is clear Sor María planned to write about all the heavens, not just one.

Another possibility is that Sor María originally left the piece unfinished, not completing it until a later time in her life, probably when she wrote the two prologues and polished the entire treatise. In fact, the 1724 manuscript meticulously prepared for Don Juan Isidro Yáñez Faxardo shows not only grammatical corrections and improvements that might be from the hand of a copy editor, but the recasting of whole paragraphs and even the introduction of new themes, both sorts of changes with an authentically Agredan flavor. This latter manuscript (designated "F") also offers the advantage of preserving intact phrases that in the seventeenth-century copies have been truncated, thereby weakening the sense and syntax of the sentence. For these reasons, then, although the text offered is from A, and completed from K, at times I have substituted or complemented with a reading from F. Although this version of *Face of the Earth*, drawn from more than one manuscript, offers the best readability in English of what Sor María probably wrote, it is not intended as a substitute for a critical edition in Spanish (which I hope to publish soon) with a systematic comparison of variant phrases. However, I have indicated in the notes almost all of the differences among the manuscripts.

3

Text of *Face of the Earth and Map of the Spheres*

B ook of Mother María de Jesús, religious sister and late abbess of the Conceptionist convent of the town of Agreda, dealing with the face of the world, the elements and a little about the heavens. This book was found in Madrid, the original belonging to Father Salizanes, bishop of Córdoba, from whom Señor Samaniego, bishop of Plasencia, was able to have made just one copy, which reads as follows.

Chapter 5

About the first degree of illumination, and the knowledge of the face of the whole earth and its inhabitants that my soul received through mystical knowing, along with some hidden secrets of the earth.

W onderful is the Lord as seen in the face of the earth, in having created it and in the providence with which He cares for it, and in its orderly arrangement. What a good dish to set before this magnificent King and Lord! And what grand and delicious fare for the palate of the guest, who is mankind wandering here below, if only we would let ourselves enjoy it! And what a good reason to praise the Creator of such a structure, the giver of life to the universe! The shame is that all mortal creatures might well

keep the image of the earth in mind but do not do so for two insur-
mountable reasons, and so we do not repay such a great kindness.

The first reason is its immense size, its length, and breadth. Since
we, as creatures, are limited, we cannot understand it, not knowing it
beyond a certain part, familiar only with the space within which we
live and move. Secondly, since one cannot comprehend or grasp this
wonder, texts are not prepared, the subject is not presented to the
mind, nor is information supplied in such a way as to move one's will
to love the Lord, through whom and from whom we receive this beneficial kindness.

I feel the Lord has given me light to know the truth of this so that
by knowing I might leave behind my ignorance and, having been well
schooled by experience, find it does me good, like a medicine to make
not only me better but my brothers and sisters, too, for I would like
them to share what I have learned and experienced.[1] Now one cannot
deny the many marvels I have received from the generous hand of the
Most High, and that is a compelling reason to recognize Him as the
Creator of all He has shown me and so to serve Him, for He is a marvelous and magnificent God, and to praise Him for all that He does on
behalf of such a poor, lowly creature.

The first wonder His Highness showed me—among the countless
number I know myself unable to describe—was the earth. And everything the Lord showed me was done just as I shall explain, and to
make it all clearer, I shall follow the order of events as the Lord brought
them about. I found myself in contemplation after having received
the most holy sacrament and given thanks, when there appeared a
holy angel, exceedingly beautiful and delightful. He said to me, "May
the Lord be your eternal well-being and give life to your spirit, my
dear. His Highness wants you to entrust yourself to Him. He keeps his
promises faithfully; his word is less likely to fail you than the heavens
and the earth. His Majesty wishes to keep his promise to give you
mystical knowledge of all things. He will reveal great mysteries to
you and commands for that purpose that you come into his presence,
that is, standing above all things created and in the presence of God
alone." And although we always are there, still this was by means of
a vision from the Lord perceived by my intellect, accompanied by specific experiences.

As soon as I said, "The will of His Highness be done,"[2] He said to me, "My wife and turtledove, I created the heavens and the earth and the elements and the sea. I want you to know the purpose for which all that has being was created and of my watchful providence that protects mankind, and that I have provided for it many kindnesses and a diversity of created things. Pay attention and look." I looked carefully. I did as the Most High commanded, and I saw what is impossible for me to explain, something of which my mind had known nothing. My understanding was through the illumination of revelation, without which, by natural means, it could not have come about. So that I might see and know and understand, the Lord endowed me with a special ability (and that in itself was another of his great marvels), in order that I might know all the face of the earth, the sea, some of the big rivers, the animals, the inhabitants, the cities and kingdoms, and the diversity of creatures—all these things—and still its being so big was not an obstacle. And while there is no denying its size—even though by natural means one cannot see a quarter of a league ahead—still I was able to know and form an opinion of the smallest things, for my sight extended many, many leagues distant, as far away as the earth stretches. I saw the diverse creatures there are within it, along with other aspects of it, as though all these things were no farther from me than a crossbow shot; and I will tell now just how distinctly I perceived it all.

I saw the earth and its immensity, which I found truly astonishing, though no more than all I perceived within it. I could see, then, that the earth is divided into four parts, and beneath each of the meridians that separate it in this way there is a dwelling,[3] the relationship among the four of them being somewhat symmetrical.

The first of these four parts is the one in which we live, though any one may be considered the first of the four dwellings I am now describing. It does not matter which one you start counting with; it comes out the same. The second dwelling is of the people called or known as the Perioecians, which means they live in that other section or region of the earth. The third dwelling is of the people known as the Antoecians, which are, and whose name means, those who live opposite us. The fourth dwelling is of the people who are known and called the Antipodes. Their dwelling is contrary to where we are, so situated that their feet are directly opposite to ours; our nadir is their zenith, and our zenith is their nadir. And if we think and say that they are upside down, they can say the same about us.

But the truth of the matter is, and this I have seen and recognized, is that we are all right side up; we should not judge on the basis of our own situation who is right side up, but in relation to the center of the earth and the world. Everyone's feet point down toward the center, which is their foundation, while their heads go up toward the sky, and so both they and we are straight up, just the way God wants and commands it to be, each group living where its lot fell to it. Divine providence arranged for mankind to have our heads up to the sky and our feet on the earth so that we should know and be aware that we were born from the earth and formed from it, though our final home will not be on the earth. On pleasures and vanities we must step, denying them all and not giving ourselves over to them for our delight; that is why our feet were placed on it. Instead we should long for our country, which is Heaven, and meditate on it day and night and look toward it; that is the reason they put our heads toward that heavenly Jerusalem for which we were created. That is why our feet go down to the earth and our heads up to the sky.

The Antipodes and we do not share the same seasons, for when they have summer, we have winter, and when we have day, they night; and when we have the longest day of the year, they have the longest night and the shortest day. And this is true, for I saw it was so. And it is a great wonder of the Most High to see the night in one part of the world and the day in another, in some parts the sun and in others the moon, the moon and the shadow caused by the absence of the sun, for the world is like a ball. Seen all together, it offered a beautiful diversity and revealed its Author to be a great and magnificent King.

To give a clearer idea of how the world was shown to me, let me say it was by reproducing images of it for me, so that I might see it in God. I saw it so clearly that it all seemed to spring from God. In His Highness I perceived all the images. I cannot be sure of the exact way in which I saw them. But the world is divided into four parts; to make myself clear I will describe them in order, and they are Europe, Asia, Africa, and America.

The structure and body of the earth is so large that its circumference alone is 9,280 leagues, as I perceived.[4] The part already discovered is 8,480 leagues.[5] The 800 remaining are an island near the two poles called Arctic and Antarctic. At the time of the apostles it was uninhabited, empty of every sort of people, and so the Gospel has not been preached there.

Closer to our own time on this island, in the year of the Lord 700, a people migrated toward this part of the world, a people so vicious that no one could tolerate them, and they settled on this island. They multiplied, acting like animals as they reproduced. About their customs I will speak later, in the part about America.[6]

The earth's diameter is 2,502 leagues, and in half of that, which is to the middle where hell is, there are 1,251 leagues of depth. At this center and heart of the earth are hell, purgatory, and limbo, hell in the middle, purgatory to one side, and limbo to the other.

Hell holds many caverns and stone mansions. It is all one infernal cavern with a mouth, and it is certain fact that there is a flat stone bigger than the mouth of hell, with a thickness of half a league, with which the mouth of hell will be covered, and on the last day the damned will be left entombed and sealed within, never to come out through all eternity.

Purgatory has a sort of licking flames, a fire from God's power that afflicts the bodiless souls, though the fire has body and substance. In limbo are visible the footprints where Christ placed his feet when He went to free the souls of the holy fathers whom He took with him. In limbo are the children who die unbaptized, whose existence is pure mystical meditation given by God, and there are some who died quite old without ever having offended God.

This land is inhabited by various sorts of people, and the Most High cares for them all at the same time, giving them life and its spark, without which they are unable to do the least of their deeds and actions. In God they move, in His Highness they live, in His Majesty they are both refreshed and vexed. He sees to them all, the righteous and the sinners. How astonishing is the diversity of these creatures, in both their actions and their inclinations as well as their outer appearance. Some are drawn to God, heeding and loving Him, some to his creatures, others to their appetites, which they pursue. Some are more perfect, others less. Some are friends of the Most High, some of the devil. Some are pleasing to God for their grace, others abominable for their sin.

By the diversity of their outer appearance one cannot know their inner qualities, for there are some who are courteous, having good inclinations, being clean and beautiful, but still ignorant; others who are not as good looking are intelligent and wise. The Spanish are of a goodly appearance, the French, English, and Germans better, just as energetic but less educated. In Europe there are a variety of elegant if curious ways of dressing, many pleasing manners, and the peoples are handsomely formed, although some by diseases have become misshapen. Africans, Asians, and Americans are short of stature and almost hairy. What they wear are skins, cut and painted in bizarre ways. While some are misshapen, others are deformed by being so tall, even as much as three yards—some more than four or six and the absolute tallest eight[7]—and some are very brutish. There are also dwarves about half a yard high,[8] such being the extreme diversity of creatures and such the greatness of the Most High.

Very different sorts of people live in the other parts of the world. In the vicinity of the Indies, they wear a sort of earrings from their noses, lips, and chins, made of stones, though not as well crafted and set in jewelry as in Spain. On other islands there are people with ears so long they reach the ground.[9] There is such a number of creatures that to our mind they seem uncountable. And one should notice carefully that while there are so many, still none are alike, not in their natures, their faces, their bodies, or their inclinations, or in their social organizations and governments, for each kingdom is different.

It is also very worth noticing the hierarchy they have, some standing above others, such as the kings above the grandees, the grandees above the lords, the more distinguished knights from the lesser ones. Some are big, others small: lords, husbandmen, slaves. All of this is much to the glory of their Creator, as is the diversity of the various lesser occupations in which each one is engaged. The rich are terribly ambitious, and that is a poison that neither rich nor poor escape. And more so in our own time, when there is no truth or faithfulness or concern for fairness. All is madness, vanity of vanities, and hollow words, especially those who blindly worship false gods.

David was right in saying that all people lie. Mankind's life on earth is a struggle and like the morning dew that soon is gone, like the flower of the field that quickly withers. We mortals are so blind that out of such a multitude of people only a small portion know the true God, primarily in this part of the world, Europe, the Spaniards being the most faithful. Among those raised in the church, few confess the faith and many of them are in sin, so nineteen out of twenty parts of mankind live in darkness and blindness.

Idolatry had its origin[10] at the time of Abraham. What led to it was that the son of a very rich man, whom he loved most tenderly, died very young; to console himself the man had a statue made in his image and commanded his servants to worship and offer it sacrifices belonging rightly and properly only to God. This went on and the vice was made a law. Later Nin,[11] a descendent of Cain (Noah's bad son), king of Babylon and the founder of Ninevah (that Genesis calls Assur), made a statue of his father Belo, placed it in a temple he had built in Babylon, and commanded that he be worshiped like a God. From this comes the fact that some idols are called gods, being given names such as Bel, Baal, Balin, Belphegor.[12] In some provinces, statues were raised to kings by subjects of theirs who felt they governed well.

For this reason or other causes they find compelling, some peoples worship the sun and the moon. The Memphians worship the ox; the Mendesians worship the goat; the Scythians and the Lamians the bee; the Quipolitans the wolf; the Zinopolitans the dog; the Traodens mice.[13] Europe, which is the best of the four parts of the world, is the most fortunate, the one God has blessed.

The second part is called Africa, the third Asia, the fourth America, and I will go into each of these four in all the detail with which they were revealed to me. And so I might better understand what the world is, it was shown to me either in images or seeing it in God. I saw it so clearly that everything seems to spring from God. In His Highness I perceived all the images, but I cannot be sure in what way I could see it.

It is something wonderful and a source of great amazement to see the immensity of this world so full of mountains and plains and valleys and bad lands; other parts are very pleasant, offering many sorts of flowers, plant, and fruits for an ungrateful mankind. There are some inhabitable parts of the world, others that are not. Some parts of this structure are densely populated by diverse and different sorts of people—some Christians, others that are not and do not know God, fleeing from the light and the truth; and in other parts they love and value the Lord. And there is a diverse and uneven variety of people, some living in great solitude. In some parts there are very Catholic people who confess the faith; in other parts they dismiss it, while in others they do not know it. There are so many differences and kinds of people it is impossible to state them all.

Oh, most high, immortal King, uncreated and sole creator of all that has being! May your immense majesty be praised, my Lord and my King, for your marvelous providence in creating this structure and wonder that is the world with such a multitude of adornments and diversity of plants, flowers, fruits, animals, and birds that in it are sustained by the waters; and such a variety of fish; so many herbs with healing power in them for mankind. And if our ignorance were not so great and our knowledge so limited, what marvelous secrets of nature that now Your Highness has hidden would you show us and we would learn.

Oh, boundless wisdom! I do not know whether to be more astonished at the diversity of plants and animals and other things or at the fact that each of them You sustain, fill with life and being according to its own needs and purposes. I do not know whether to be more amazed at the meticulous care, protection, purposefulness, and love with which You provide them to mankind, or at the fact that Your Highness will tolerate our ungratefulness, the bad repayment we make, and the thoughtlessness we show about so many and such generous kindnesses. And how big they are, my Most High Lord, the earth and all the many animals sustained on it and hidden in its huts and caves! So many birds fly through the air, so many fish are contained and nourished within its watery lodges, and all for the delight of an ungrateful mankind!

How I wish I could make the proper payment and offer the praises due so many mercies and favors! I offer them up for us travelers here below and beg the blessed in Heaven to do the same, for we mortals have such sluggish hearts, are creatures made and shaped from the slime of the earth. Let the angels, seraphim, and the blessed always praise you and say, "Holy, holy, holy is the Lord of the heavenly hosts, worthy of praise and reverence and a new song."

Saints, you who already enjoy seeing the face of the Most High and are in Heaven, for you see Him in the fullness of knowing and so are able to judge truly the worth of the kindnesses we travelers below receive yet through our ignorance and indolence do not recognize— praise the Lord, bless Him, and as you offer up those praises remember the kindnesses given to his slave and servant, María. Offer up payment on behalf of this poor, lowly creature for the countless benefits I receive through no merit of my own. May He be eternally praised. Amen.

Chapter 6

About the first of the four parts of the world, called Europe, and about some of its kingdoms and provinces and certain other mysteries that divine providence has accomplished, revealing itself more in this part of the world than in the other three, for here the holy faith is confessed in Spain.

Europe's western boundary is the great sea, which is called the Atlantic Ocean; on the north it is bounded by the English and German Sea; to the south it is closed in by the Mediterranean Sea; on the east is the Tanais River,[14] which the Scythians[15] call Silim, and Lake Maeotis,[16] which the same people call Themerida, meaning almost "the sea's mother." It is more illustrious than Asia or Africa or America; but it is not as broad. Nowhere is it 222 German miles wide, except toward the north and south where it spreads itself out as though it had dragon wings, and its greatest width is in those wings. Its length extends from the Tanais River to the Strait of Gibraltar, almost 750 German miles.

The westernmost region of Europe is Spain, which contains three provinces:[17] Betica, which is called Andalucia, within which is the kingdom of Granada; Lusitania, that now is called the kingdom of Portugal; Tarraconensis, which is divided into many kingdoms— Galicia, Navarre, and Castile, in which are included Leon and Aragon, and it is thought of as taking in Valencia and Catalunya. The closest place to Spain is France, the two kingdoms being separated by the Pyrenees.

That explains that on the west France is separated from Spain by mountains. On the east the Rhine River separates it from Germany. As for the other sides, on the north the boundary is the Ocean Sea,[18] while on the south the Mediterranean Sea. It is divided into four parts, which are Aquitania, Lugdunum, Belgium, and Narbo,[19] the latter separated from the rest of France by the Cevennes and Jura mountains and extending all the way to the sea. Those who inhabit the region of the Rhine are the peoples of Upper and Lower Germany, and from them over to the Sarmatians,[20] it is all called Germany. On the north it is bordered by the Ocean Sea along a nearly straight coast, except near Dania,[21] which sometimes is called Dacia. There an arm of land sticks out into the sea called the Chersonese.[22] On the south it ends at the Alps. It is a fertile land, and in this part very populous and abundant. In it there are mighty rivers, such as the Rhine, the Neckar, the Elbe, and the Danube, which empties into the sea through seven mouths. This is a most beautiful river, and of all others, this one filled me with wonder at its great size. There are many other rivers.

Germany is divided into Swabia, Franconia, Thuringia, Vogtland, and Vindelicia,[23] which is part of Bavaria. Toward the south is Moravia,[24] which is connected to Upper Pannonia,[25] which in turn is called the Archduchy of Austria. Then comes lower Pannonia, which today is called Hungary. Then comes Moesia,[26] over to the sea from the Danube. In between is Bohemia,[27] and next to it the Hercinian Forest.[28] To the north is Misna,[29] Saxony, and after those toward the Rhine are Westphalia, Hessia, Hartz, Friesland,[30] Holland. On the other side of Saxony are Holstein, Silesia,[31] the Mark,[32] Mecklenburg, Pomerania,[33] which reaches all the way to Sarmatia. The peoples of Sarmatia are Lithuanians, Poles, Wallachians,[34] Transylvanians.[35] Then come Dacia,[36] followed by Thrace, which is now called Greece and divided into the following regions: Epirus, Achaia, Macedonia, and Morea. The Dalmatians[37] and Illyrians[38] that today are called Slavonia[39] surround the Adriatic Sea. Farther on is Italy with its provinces: Campania, Calabria, Puglia, Tuscany, Umbria, Gallia Togata,[40] Lombardy, Venice, and the province of Ancona.

After seeing this part of the world, the angel said the following words: "Look carefully, soul, at all these provinces, places, and kingdoms, for the Lord is to be marveled at for the diversity and quantity of peoples. Look and observe, my dear, that Europe is the smallest of the four parts of the world, but in it the marvels and special protection of the Most High shine the brightest. In this part, which is Europe, live the Christians, the Catholic faith is confessed, the uncreated God is worshiped and reverenced, and its inhabitants, though they often offend Him, are Christians, at least most of them. But the church militant is based in this part of the world, and for that reason it is and always has been fortunate. And among the Catholics who form the heart of the church militant—I mean those who live in this part of the world—the Lord has many holy friends of his, in whom can be seen the Most High's very generous gifts of the spirit.

"When His Majesty created the world and gave it his blessing, He paid special attention to Europe and particularly to Spain. His Highness gave it the best climate and made it a pleasant land suitable for human habitation. It is rich in all things that support mankind but are lacking in the rest of the world, for Our Lord gave it his blessing and looked kindly on it. It is a greater and truer gift than the one Isaac gave to Jacob, for Isaac was fooled when he touched Jacob's hairy hands and thought they were Esau's. But this true Father was not deceived, for He cannot be, yet although deceit is not in fact practiced on Him, still out of compassion He allows Himself to seem to be deceived. So although He knew that the Christians who live in this part of the world would not be faithful children and did not deserve a blessing, for they would commit many offenses against His Highness, still so that He might give them his blessing, He covered their bad deeds with the skin of his faithful son Jesus Christ, and weighing in his mind who He was, what He would suffer and that He was to put on human nature, He was won over and gave his generous blessing.

"The part of the sky and the planets that give light to Europe are very well tempered, for which reason the people are intelligent, courageous, and vigorous. They are more civilized than anywhere else in

the world. Their stature and appearance are the best, their monar-
chies better administered, their rulers more respected. And although
it is true that all of Europe is like that, still Spain is even more fortunate; its king should be the most grateful, for he has received the
most. When it comes to all different kinds of people, Europe is very
different from Asia, Africa, and America. When one knows just how
true that is, the differences can be seen to be like those separating
Heaven from earth, men from angels, and animals from men; it is a
strange and astonishing subject, as I shall explain later.

"In the regions of Europe that border on the other three parts of the
world there are, through the contact with those parts, very bestial
and bizarre people. The most fortunate place of all, where there is the
least mixture of heresy, is Spain, which was the land blessed by the
God of Zion who created the heavens and the earth. To it we can apply the words of the prophet Samuel: 'You will go up to the mountain
of God where there is a band of Philistines, and at the entrance to the
city, a company of prophets coming down from on high will come out
to meet you. They will carry musical instruments: psaltery, tambou-
rine, flute, and zither. They will be prophesying, and then the spirit
of the Lord will come upon you, and you will prophesy with them
and become another man.'[41]

"This happened to the Catholics of the holy church. They went to
the mountain of God, in the sense of being born into the church,
where the holy faith is confessed. While growing to become children
of the church, they encountered a squadron of Philistines, who are the
devils, always alert, and the unbelievers who in their wrath attack
the ship of the church. But God is so compassionate that at the entrance to the city, that is, as soon as we accept the faith, He offers us
a company of prophets, who are the saints and their descendants. Although founded and formed on earth, it comes from on high, for every gift and present has its origin there, and its members were able to
do all things in the Lord who comforts them, for whoever confesses
the faith is armed with this shield. So they come down, descending
like the spirit from above. They bring musical instruments that are
their prophecies and the mild law of the Most High, instruments leading us to follow their example.

"No one can imagine, unless she has experienced it, what joy and harmony it brings the heart to hear the prophecies of the saints and to put them in practice. Those who do not confess this faith live in darkness and bitterness. Those who do confess it walk in the light because they follow the Lord and take pleasure in his mild law and the musical instruments played by the saints."

Oh, my most high Lord! How can I, an unworthy, lowly creature, repay the kindness Your Highness has done me by showing me these mysteries? And how can I satisfy the desire to love You that I feel when I think about something so great? While still in the flesh of this mortal life, how can my will withstand the spurs of my understanding when I understand such immense ideas, or of my memory when I remember them? It would have been better for my life to have ended so that my repayment might be that offered by a blessed soul in Heaven and not what can be given by a poor soul burdened with suffering. Let them praise You, Most High, all the blessed who delight in seeing your face, and would that I were free of the chains and shackles of mortal existence, at which my spirit so sorely chafes.

My Lord, break these chains or close my eyes to these many wonders You show me. I recognize, my King, that You have done me a wonderful favor by placing me within the company of the Catholic faith and the church militant. What language, my love, might there be to express all the wonder of these tender mercies I receive from Your Highness? May You be eternally praised by all your creatures. Amen.

[Chapter 7][42]

Second part of the world, called Africa, and what the Most High showed me about it.

Africa took its name from a descendent of Abraham and his wife, Cetura[43]; he came to Libya, which is what the Greeks call Africa, and he came with an army. After defeating his enemies, he established himself, making his home there. Africa begins at the Strait of Gibraltar and ends at the Egyptian Sea, to the north bounded by the Mediterranean Sea and to the south by the Ethiopian Sea.[44] It has many provinces: first the Mauritanias,[45] Tangerine,[46] and Caesarean,[47] plus Numidia.[48] These three together are now called Barbary. It has, too, Libya, which includes Carthage, Byzacene, and Cyrene,[49] the latter known also as Pentapolis.[50] It has, too, Egypt and Ethiopia.

Tangerine Mauritania has the Mallow River[51] on its eastern border, to the north the Spanish Sea and the strait, to the west the Atlantic Sea. In this province there is a mountain called Abila,[52] one of the two Columns of Hercules. There are other mountains, called the Seven Sisters. Caesarean Mauritania is situated between Tangerine Mauritanea, to its west, Numidia to its east, and the Mediterranean Sea to its north. Farther on, in the Carthaginian region, beginning with the Ampsaga River,[53] is Numidia. The inhabitants of this province carry their houses in carts, just as they do in the German province of Misnia to make it easy to graze their cattle in more favorable and fertile places.

Then there is another province called Africa proper, making use of the same name given to the whole region; it contains the following cities: Zeusis, Carthage, Maxula, and Utica, where Cato died.[54] Then comes Byzacene. Nearby is a city called Hadrumetum,[55] and another called Leptis,[56] and the Cynips River,[57] and a region called Tripolitana,[58] having three cities, and among them is Leptis or Naples (not the one in the European region). Near here is Syrtis Major.[59] At the place farthest from the coast, there are some boundaries or limits called the Arae Philaenorum.[60] Next comes the province of Cyrene. To its south are the Garamantes[61] and the Ethiopians, to the north the Libyan Sea and a place called the town of Catabathmos.[62] From there to the north is Marmarica,[63] known also as Libya Mareotis. It borders on Egypt, the province near the Nile River. On the east are grouped Judea, Arabia Petrea,[64] and the Red Sea, or Arabian Gulf, while to the north is the Egyptian Sea and to the south the Ethiopian Sea. In this region, the holy angels told me, it does not rain; but in the dog days of high summer the River Nile overflows, leaving the land fertile. So it is through God's great providence that it does not rain; he commands the river to overflow for the good of these provinces.

The best-known cities are Alexandria, head of all Egypt, and Cairo, or Babylon. With these two goes Memphis. Below Egypt is Ethiopia.

In the east is the region of the Troglodytes.[65] In this region the inhabitants are more animals than people. Here live the Aegipanes[66] and the Blemyes,[67] headless people, though they really are not but have it stuck in their chests between high shoulders. The appearance of these people is bizarre, with their eyes in their chests. I learned that some Spaniards have thought these people to be headless, but they are not, but simply have it the way I have said. They are very bright people, though lacking education, for that is something they make little use of. If they did, they would be quick learners and good at it. They are short and stocky; what they look like is tree stumps.

Here the Satyrs[68] live without houses or anything else civilized, just like beasts in the field; they are bad looking. And some of the inhabitants of this land have something like bumps or horns—I do not know what to call them—that make them repulsive. They grow out of their foreheads and go back to a time when some of their ancestors were abused on their foreheads because they were not Christians, but they did not suffer it for God but simply in obedience to their cruel law, which required a perverse ceremony in which they were struck a certain number of times. That is how they came to have this bulge or big callous.[69] This senseless torture still goes on.

There are others they call Cynocephalians,[70] whose faces are like dogs because their snouts stick out so much. Their faces are very narrow, with sunken cheeks, and their bodies badly shaped. Most of them walk on four feet and lie down on the ground like animals. There are others who have only one eye[71] where the two normally come together, and pug noses.[72] The face is grotesquely wide, and all of them have bodies unpleasant to look at because they are so ugly. The shame of it is that they are God's creatures like us, but whether with one eye or two, they will not enter into the kingdom of Heaven (should we wish to take the gospel literally)[73] but with just one into hell, for they neither love nor know their Creator and Lord. These are foul-smelling and impure creatures. Their gaze is always fixed, looking foolishly toward the heavens; they look at that wonder, but they will never be able to enjoy it. They are called Monoculars.[74] They are blind and stupid, unable to talk.[75]

There is a sort of a plague on this region, which is the presence of many dragons, rhinoceri, tigers, basilisks, and a wide variety of other sorts of animals and snakes. In this region there are lots of other poisonous vermin. Likewise in Africa, though on the side opposite from the one I have just described, there live many elephants, unicorns, and other animals that, even though they are not human, are more pleasant to see than some of the people from these provinces.

Oh, how great are the deeds of the Most High, my King. I am left stuttering and unable to pronounce any word at all when my heart reflects on how many thanks and praises it owes to Your Highness for having created me as I am, my King, when there are so many barbarians and benighted peoples. They have souls like mine and five senses. The infinite price in your most holy[76] blood that I cost, they cost, too, and are worth the same. In your image and likeness You created them, my King, as You did the other creatures.

Who, most high and uncreated God, asked You more for me than for them? Before You created us, who obliged you, my Lord, to make me one of the called and one of those who confess the holy faith, when there are so many who, if they should have been so lucky, would have served You better than I, valuing and reverencing better the holy mysteries of the gospel law and showing more gratitude? Was it perhaps because You did not know, Lord and magnificent King, the bad return that I would make You, my bad and disordered life? No, indeed, because from *ab initio* Your Majesty knows who all the travelers through this world will be. And as I would turn out to be the most wretched and ungrateful of them all, you would have seen through me all the better.

Oh, infinite God! May Your Majesty be eternally praised for such great and unspeakable favors, as are confessing the faith and your holy law, so gentle and mild, just and holy, pure and clean, pleasant and wise. It is not subject to errors or not knowing. It is true and strong, bitter for transgressors, sweet and smooth for those who confess it, bitter and hard to bear for those who scorn it. All good is bound up within it, it has no evil at all.

You are, my Lord, its author, and so it is the law of the God of Abraham and Isaac and Jacob, whose head is Christ, its treasure[77] and ransom his most holy blood. May You be eternally blessed, my Lord, for this law that You have given to your servants. Powerful, holy, and strong, a knife against heretics, destroyer of idols, shadow that terrifies hell, refreshment and relief to those who live beneath its protection and aid, unfailing in rewarding, consoling, and giving life to its chosen ones, standing above all law without stain or spot or wrinkle, for it cannot be blemished or contain any lie.

Chapter 8

About the third part of the world, which is called Asia, and what I saw regarding it in the light given me through his kindness by the Most High Lord.

The ocean touches Asia on three sides: on the south it is the Indian Sea, on the north the Scythian Sea,[78] and on the east the Eastern Sea. On the west, Asia is next to Africa and Europe, and the Mediterranean Sea, which is between the other two. In this part of the world there is a great diversity in human appearance and a variety of social customs. Some people wear sashes or stoles, which are kinds of garments, for basically they go naked and use them only for decoration. There are others who have long ears. There are many who are extremely white and so come to be covered with something like a red down formed by freckles; they are so completely enveloped in it that they look like leather-skinned animals. There are others who are tall, skinny giants, ugly and stretched out of all proportion. Farther on there are some dwarves who look like they have been cooked up out of the earth, no more than half a yard high. They are very cute because the Most High shaped their bodies with the normal proportions. They look like funny little toys, and to think that one Lord created them all is more than enough reason to be amazed and recognize his power. There are others that have no legs, just big arms and small bodies and big heads. They walk with their arms and bodies, looking like tree stumps and three-footed animals, for their arms seem like two feet and their bodies a third. But that is not what they are, but rational beings. This is a fertile and abundant land. There are many peoples, but what astonishes me about it is the diversity of the people.

The places in Asia and this part of the world are like this. The first province next to that of Asia proper[79] is Pontus and Bythinia. Then the provinces of Cappadocia, Lycia, Caria, Pamphylia, Mysia,[80] and Armenia, where the Tigris and Euphrates run toward the south. Then come the Cappadocians (who are called the Pontics) and the Amazons,[81] (who are long-breasted and throw them over their shoulders), the Sarmatians along the Tanais River, and the Scythians last of all. Surrounding the Caspian Sea are the Caspians, the Medes,[82] and the Hyrcanians.[83] The Parthians,[84] Carmanians,[85] and Persians are on the Persian Gulf. The Babylonians, Mesopotamians, and Syrians to the south. The Arabs are on the Arabian Gulf. After Turkey is Aria,[86] Paropamisus,[87] Drangiana,[88] Gedrosia.[89] After that is India, with the Ganges River between its two halves.

In the south of this part of the world, there is a great diversity of peoples, all of them different, so much that their diversity is a reason to praise the Most High. They show little mercy to each other, harming each other terribly and waging wars continuously. I perceived that a terrible demon, a schemer, has his headquarters there. This is the demon who has provoked conflict in the world and is now present where the biggest ones rage. They eat human flesh,[90] and to roast it, I saw with my own eyes that they impaled a live boy on a stick, and there were many of them there, and when he moaned, they jumped and grunted so as not to hear him. But the worst of it is that this was not done out of compassion, but is a ceremony they have to celebrate the meal. As I was asking myself who or whose that boy might be to let that happen to him, I understood that it is a law and custom of theirs to give up one out of five children.

I also understood that it had been an order of the Most High for me to see the world at this time. They fight with some heavy iron clubs. No group of people is worse, in my opinion, than this one, for I intensely hate the absence of peace and brotherly love. They dispute with the griffins[91] for the metal gold, struggling to obtain it.

In this land in the region of Mount Imaus,[92] there are savages deformed by having their feet reversed. They run a lot. There are others with faces like dogs, and instead of speaking, they growl or bark. Others have only one leg and with the foot, which is big and round, they protect themselves from the weather by lifting it up high. They lie on the ground and are called Sciapodes.[93]

In this part there are creatures that some people here have thought to be without mouths or eyes,[94] but that is not right, for they do have them. The fact is that close to the eyelashes or eyelids there are some little curtains given them by nature. When they need to do something, they raise them, and when not, they are able to see with the light that comes through them, more than enough for walking. Their mouths have the upper lip[95] so long that it goes down to the chin. These are ridiculous creatures. Next to the River Ganges is where they are, and then the pygmies, and countless other kinds of people.

Oh, deepest wisdom and divine painter! Who is not amazed and inspired to see the variety of creatures You created, the inclinations Your Highness gave them, how You look and call to them all, my God, whenever they are willing to turn their eyes to You? How astonishing Your Majesty's goodness, for even when they do not heed You, still You bear it, not annihilating them but sustaining and giving them life? Eternal blessings on You for giving me the law of love and commanding that we love each other like ourselves, keeping some from becoming the food of others. My dear and my Lord, even if your law did not give a reason and a justification for our loving our neighbors as ourselves, in itself that precept gives reason enough to know and value your law as holy and pure and its Author as the Lord and uncreated God, Creator of all things. Only Your Highness is God of gods and Lord of lords, for the others are only wooden and metal gods who speak words of eternal death, deceitful and leading to the deepest darkness. But You, Lord, are the true light and eternal brightness.

No less am I amazed, my King, at the power of your word and the obedience of the holy angels, your ministers and my lords. You ordered that every creature should have a watchful guardian angel, and although it might well be burdensome to accompany such beastly and horrible people, still Your Highness ordered your angels to protect their paths and highways, and those princes obey and do so; I do not know what may move them except obedience, and that is what they replied when I asked them about it. But still they are not denied seeing your face and that must make them happy. Great is your goodness and compassion. May You be forever praised for such goodness and magnificence. Amen.

Chapter 9

About the fourth part of the world, which is called America, and what I understood about it and the diversity of creatures there are on this island.

America is almost entirely an island, for the sea surrounds it on most sides. It is a land very rich in gold and precious stones. It lacks many metals that we have here in abundance, such as iron and copper, to such a degree that their weapons are made of animal teeth and jawbones. It contains many provinces, and here I will mention the principal ones, which are the Island of Paria,[96] Isabella,[97] Santa Marta,[98] Cartagena, all the way to the end, which is called God's Cape and where one finds the River Platte and Peru. The most remote provinces are Yucatán and Honduras, with New Spain,[99] which is what it is called there. It is much larger than what we call Spain here; there is no comparison. To the south one comes to Guatemala, and Nicaragua, to the west of which is found the province of New Galicia. To the northeast is Florida, which is large, and the land of codfish,[100] together with the very extensive province of Labrador, and many others that are invincible.[101]

In this part of the world, near the Arctic and Antarctic poles, there is a big piece of land the Spanish have not visited. This is the land I said I would talk about when I got to it. The island covers eight hundred leagues, and there are indescribable and incredible things in it. What the angels made clear to me is that on the island I am speaking of they do not know the true God but greatly offend Him by their evil inclinations. I already said in chapter 5 that this island was populated after the law of grace, since it was in the year 700, and the first settlers were a vicious people; then the devil deceived them and they stayed on the island, over which they have spread, and no Spaniards have come to this part of the world. That is what they told me, nor is it possible at this time.

It is densely populated, though I do not know whether I should say by humans or animals; they seem more beasts than people and rational beings, though I can state that they are because while I was marveling that they could be, an angel said to me, "Yes, they are, and they have a soul like yours." Their appearance is like that of four-footed animals, since they use their hands that way. They have long ears. They do not speak to each other, but rather grunt, communicating like that. Their hands have three fingers, like birds' feet, but they are larger. They are yellow and have a scab . . . [102] like animals, and feet. Their heads are low and round, with a small body, with long feet and arms. There is no sign of buildings or houses where they might take refuge against the weather, though they have some holes or caves in the earth they have dug, just as any other animal might do to make a place to live.

With these people there were some animals like bulls and lions, although they are not; they do not even have names, because the people have not given them any. They must have one to God, for He knows everything; I did not learn it. These animals can scarcely be told from the people, although it seemed the latter showed more respect and reverence for God. As they all looked the same, I asked the angels who accompanied me whether those brutish people realized their superiority over those animals, whether they recognized it, and whether they really were.

Those princes, the ones who always cleared up my doubts, answered me. "You will notice, dear soul, that this group of people is so brutish that they do not realize that they are superior to these animals and think they are all the same. Their being different in appearance[103] they attribute to better or worse stature or looks, something they recognize in a confused sort of way. This ignorance is not something they all suffer from, though most do, but those who understand somewhat better do not know enough to inform and teach the others. There are some who know that they are superior to the animals, but that knowledge comes to them through natural human superiority or understanding." This seems yet another marvel, for their ignorance and blindness could not be greater than to fail to know whether irrational animals are beasts and whether they themselves are the same thing.

One of the holy angels told me they feed on something that grows out of the earth due to the moistness of some rivers and the sea that is next to the island. I do not know what to compare this food to except mold or the mushrooms we have here, although there is some difference between them. They are eaten with some plants that are raised in that land, plants more bitter than the wormwood we have here. It is all miserable stuff.

They do not make things with their hands, nor do they have a kingdom or any lord or houses or anything else civilized. There is a large number of them, both big and little, and they cover themselves in various ways, according to nature's gifts, for they wear no other finery or clothing than their own body hair. Some have it one way and others another, but they all look like bears.

I perceived something remarkable, that the devil does not tempt them in words but by stirring up their passions, particularly those of anger and wrath, which in them are cruel and uncontrolled, also tempting them often to be lustful and impure. And they are known to deal with the devil, for he appears to them in different shapes that please and delight them, through the charms of outer appearance making them commit a thousand moral blunders, though they do not recognize him or have words for all this. They do have some measure of malice and evil the devil himself has taught them using signs and visions and adapting their way of speaking to his purposes. They have not been fortunate enough to learn of the divine light, for the reason already mentioned that this island was not inhabited at the time of the apostles, and though they still have not received the light of the gospel, it is impossible now, too. Regarding these peoples, I think one can use that maxim God has in his church about not throwing pearls before swine.

Oh, my God and Lord, how much I wish I could describe everything that is—and I could if I were not prevented by the subject being so large—so that such a God might be known! But it is not possible for me. This story of the world has also been shortened because telling all is not necessary. Still, on the other hand, it has not seemed proper to me to leave out the most remarkable things I observed, for they are a reason to praise the Lord. Oh, immense and uncreated God! Oh, unchanging greatness! How incomprehensible and unfathomable are your judgments, my Lord! You are the same one who created the Spanish and these people. We are all souls in your image and likeness, and it is astonishing that there should be such differences.

Oh, immortal and immense God! How I wish I could, even at the cost of my life blood, spread the holy gospel law from west to east and from north to south! Oh! How I wish I could set right and show the light to everyone who is without it so they might know the Father of all light, and so, too, that those who already have it might appreciate their good fortune and realize that by so doing they walk in light and not in darkness. Moreover, so that those who do not have it might realize they walk blindly, that they will die forever. How fortunate those whose good luck led them to know You and walk in the light, enjoying such a true, clean, and pure law. Oh, my Lord! Is there any pain to equal that I feel knowing that not all mortals recognize You as their author, and that for that reason many fail to love and reverence Your Majesty?

My Lord and my beloved, if Jeremiah dwells so much on the fact that Your Highness was not recognized by your people and that they crucified You and in place of fruit bore thorns, so, too, should it be lamented and said that there is no pain to equal what one suffers on knowing of these peoples who do not recognize You and so offend your truth, crucifying You a second and many more times.

Lord God of Israel, although I am dust and ashes and no good at all, here am I, willing to die a thousand deaths for this cause, or many more if Your Highness would only grant me them to offer up as a pleasing and faithful sacrifice. But even should it be too insignificant to be of any benefit to the travelers here below in their exile, still it would calm my burning desire, for like a wounded deer I long to go to the waters of tribulations. Though these be many, they will not slake my thirst and desire, which spring from charity and love. They can never be satisfied, for I love You, my God, and want to suffer much more than I can in fact suffer or even describe. If You do not believe me, my God, put me to the test, and I will make a full reality of these my partial desires. But should I not deserve it, may my desire kill me and I be a martyr for it and for the defense of the faith that I so value and love beyond all saying, for it is the gate to well-being and the hidden treasure beneath the truth and the unchanging good that gives and promises and contains within it eternal happiness.

Treatise on the Description of the Heavenly and Elemental Spheres from the Empyrean Heaven to the Center of the Earth[104]

Preamble

To better understand the following, one must keep in mind that everything was created by the Lord and that only His Majesty is uncreated. When we accept this truth, we will necessarily not find where the Lord was or where He had his home and dwelling, for before He created everything visible, there was nothing with any substance, not the empyrean heaven, nor the lower ones, nor the earth, nor the fields, nor any other created thing. Nor did the Most High have any need of it for Himself, for his divinity is unembodied, not taking up or occupying any space, for since it has no body, it needs neither seat nor throne, not even a Heaven to put it in. It follows that we will be obliged to believe and unavoidably recognize that Heaven and earth and all things contained in them—except only that which is God—were created by Him. He created it all; for mankind traveling here below, the earth and all the other elements, animals, and plants, while for the blessed, those who have passed through the earthly death[105] to reach eternal life, Heaven and its glory.

All of this do we creatures owe to this eternal and magnificent King. And His Majesty needed nothing for Himself, for He is without beginning or end. For countless eternities He was as glorious in his being as He is today, and yet He had no house, home, or residence, and as soon as He decided upon the creation as a measure to communicate and reveal Himself, He created a place to live for the Creator who is uncreated and has no beginning. His beginning needed no one; He is *ab eterno*. His residence is within Himself and his own being without taking up place, space, Heaven, or earth, nor did He need heavenly glory, which is something similar to the effect of his cause.

Nor did He need the saints to be blessed and glorified as He is today. Just as holy, just as strong, just as wise, just as infinite was He before creating all things as He is after having created them, for within Himself He contains all things. He is infinite in his attributes, for they exist in his infinite medium, and all these perfections did He have in the past, does have in the present, and shall have in the future, incapable of existing for any instant or any length of time whatsoever without being holy, eternal, powerful, and blessed.

All three persons of the Holy Trinity are most holy and eternal, having no beginning or end. They love each other with an everlasting, mutual love, knowing and understanding each other fully, clearly, and truly. These three persons are one true God. They were in communion among Themselves, and although alone, They suffered no solitude. Though They had no material thing, nothing was lacking for Them because in comparison to their presence, everything created seems as though it were not. And whatever exists today, if the Lord did not sustain it, would cease to be. Within Himself, He encloses such greatness and magnitude that compared to God, all things created are like a drop of water thrown into the sea; the all cannot need the nothing, the Creator the creature, the higher the lower.

The Creator that only through his free will gave being to the worm that is mankind, why did He need us, for even had He not created us, would not He still have been glorious? For in and of Himself He has the principal cause of glory, for with the sight of Him, the blessed have and will have it through all eternity. With this beatific vision, they have all their rest, satiety, comfort, pleasure, happiness, and satisfaction. For if the sight of God gives this delightful happiness to all who are in his presence, and it is sufficient through worlds without end to remove suffering from a suffering mankind, to make glorious and give satiety and satisfaction to those who suffer want and decay, then true it is that God needed nothing.

The three divine persons resolved to do (to use terms we can understand) that which They had already known and decided *ab initio* (being infinite understanding), which was to make and create angels and men in their image and likeness so that the attributes of the Most High could be communicated, especially his compassion, which is what will shine the most on the last day. These and other good things are what we creatures cannot comprehend: God created mankind while His Majesty already existed in the fullness of his infinite being.

The three divine persons resolved and conferred among Themselves about these actions, to use terms we can understand, for it goes without saying that They did not need to discuss or reach an agreement to know anything, for what the Father knows *ab initio*, the son and the Holy Spirit know, too. And all three persons understand and communicate among Themselves without there being even the possibility of anything hidden, not in words as people do, but simply by looking and understanding with the generative power of the mind, and in all three persons there is only one understanding.

They resolved to create all things. Once it is known and agreed that God in the fullness of his being and in his divine mind decided to create all things, it should be observed—since God was uncreated and within Himself—that He gave being and existence to nothing visible except following the order and manner Moses describes in the Genesis chapter. And so it may move people to praise their Creator, I here summarize the elemental and heavenly spheres, taking the information from the first part of the world, something about which I have written in greater detail and at greater length, but to make this subject handier and more useful for our understanding and fragile memory the following is sufficient.

Chapter 10

About the mystical light the Most High gave me to perceive the elemental and heavenly regions and the natures of the four elements and heavenly bodies.

The elemental region is understood to include everything contained from the sphere of the moon to the center of the earth, and is called elemental because it is entirely composed of the four elements or simple substances, which are fire, air, water, and earth. As the universal starting points and instruments that form all the mixed and compound ones, God's majesty gave them those four primary qualities so different among themselves—heat, cold, dryness, and moistness—to carry out the generation and decay of all elemental things. For this reason, we creatures are subject to these elements and diverse qualities and suffer so much through their effects.

The holy angels told me that the elements are instruments in the hand of the Most High to test and then crown the righteous, to punish the reprobates, and finally to be the scourge and just punishment for the sin of our original parents. Among the things that turned against mankind when we sinned were these elements, or to put it better, through sin we deserved and prepared ourselves for human decay, which is brought about through the four elements.

It should be observed that these four have such diverse properties that each element has two of its own, an active one with which it acts and another passive one, with which it is acted upon. Air is strong and acts on moisture, while it is acted upon by heat; the coolness of water is the property that acts, while moisture is the one that is acted upon; earth acts upon dryness and is acted upon by coolness. Regarding this diversity, I perceived and they explained to me that since they are such different properties, the result is a constant fight and struggle among the four elements striving naturally to preserve their own natures and retain the essential being God gave them, while at the same time not failing in the slightest to participate in the mixtures and combinations that naturally occur among them. And out of all these different and contrary natures, there comes a perfect harmony that with a surprising and astonishing balance configures the elemental sphere and region in its due and definite proportions.

An element is a simple substance, pure and not mixed with any other substance. This is so much so that its parts have no diversity at all, nor are they made from any others. Moreover, there is a difference between the elementary substances and the elements, for the elementary substances are composed of many things, while each element is a simple substance. Now some people have thought that the elements are dispersed into particles and so present in the mixtures and compounds, but that is not correct,[106] for the elements are not actually in the mixtures and compounds but only present through the effect of their properties. The natural and proper place and situation of the elements is for them to be on top of and surrounding each other, for the reason that all have an intrinsic tendency to move directly to their own places. In the following chapters I will explain more fully what is each element's place.

One cannot fail to recognize, my Creator and Lord, who is the Author of such marvels and that his power is infinite. Eternal God, let all the creatures praise You, for You formed them, You sustain them and take away their lives in a natural way by means of these elements, for they control and sustain, preserve and consume us. You are amazing in all things, not the least of which are these elements, and your greatness and what You bring about in them is no less to be marveled at. As their Creator and Author, You should be blessed, for with just these words, "Let the dry land stand in the midst of the waters and the waters beneath the firmament be separated from the waters over the firmament," with these so efficacious words, my God, all of the elements were created in accordance with your will and word, then formed into compounds and placed in their proper places, where they are quick to obey their Maker. They are astonishingly integrated, and such are the wonderful forces that sustain this perfect world that serves an ungrateful mankind. Most ungrateful are we, indeed, for we do not make the payment that these benefits deserve. I offer it up to You, my Lord, for all the human race, and I invite all the angelic beings (for they know what mankind does not) to offer up that praise and glory my heart longs to give and that which my so stammering tongue neither dares nor knows how to utter.

Chapter 11

About the first element, which is earth, and what the Lord has shown me and where it is.

Earth is naturally cold and dry. It is dense and very heavy, for which reason its natural place is in the middle of the universe, in all directions the most distant place from Heaven. With his providence, God sustains it, and contrary to what some false prophets have said, it is not sustained by any other force, for that is something no one can give except the true God and Lord, Creator of the universe.

The earth together with its waters makes a round, spherical body, and although on the earth there are highs and lows, mountains and valleys, they do not really affect the earth's roundness, for compared with the whole they are smaller than grains of sand. I saw the proof that this is true one morning when the sun was rising, for as it rose, it shone first on the eastern peoples[107] and then little by little began to show itself to those in the west. What one concludes is that the earth and water form a round body, for if it were otherwise, the instant the sun came up it would be seen by half the world, assuming the latter to be flat, and every shadow imitates the shape of the object that produces it. From this, one infers that the earth has a circular shape.

It has a circumference of 9,280 leagues,[108] while the diameter, as has been said, is 2,502 leagues. To the place where hell, purgatory, and limbo are, the distance is 1,251 leagues, and that location, as well as the holy places where the Lord shed his blood, are in the middle of the earth. Purgatory is beneath Mount Calvary, with hell on one side and limbo on the other, as will be explained when it is time. The thickness of the earth from Mount Calvary to purgatory is 1,251 leagues.

This body and element, the earth, is, as I have said, the first, since it is the heaviest. It contains three regions: in the first grow fruit, trees, and plants that nourish the animals, while in turn the animals and plants nourish mankind. In this region, fountains gush out, rivers run, mountains rise up, and volcanoes erupt. This zone does not extend below the surface more than seven times the height of a person.

In the second region are generated the earth's vapors and warm breaths through the energy and power of the sun's rays, as transmitted through its influence and that of the planets. Here all the metals are formed: gold, silver, copper, iron, bronze, tin, lead, mercury, and the minerals that can be ground, such as sulphur, alum, copperas, and vitriol.

In the third region of the earth, nothing is produced because it is true that the energy that generates and creates all things does not reach so deep. And so in this last region the earth is purer and simpler. Its quakes and tremors, when they occur, are generated within the second zone and result from the many breaths produced in its deepest cavities, breaths that contain in concentrated form the energy of rays from the sun, stars, and planets, for since these are not free there to rise through the air, they shake the earth, causing many quakes in those places where they occur.

On the earth live a large number of animals that it supports. I will remark here on the most remarkable ones I observed. Out of all the countless parts of creation I saw, they seemed to surpass the others in their beauty and their secrets of nature. Among the animals I saw a marvel of a bird,[109] delightful to look at. This bird lives around the Mediterranean Sea in the third part of the world—Asia, in its western part. It was shown to me so I might praise its Creator. What most impressed me was its beauty and large size, which exceed that of a peacock. It has a long neck, while its head is decorated with feathers of varied and most beautiful colors; the wings are similar to the feathers in the headdress, and when the sun shines on it, its many hues shine like enamel over gold and silver. I saw it at a time when it was caring for two of its little children. And nature has given it so much maternal love that with wings outstretched, she stood around them, making a wall to defend them from the waves of the sea; since it is so close by, she raises them with much anxiety, the faithful mother locked in combat with the very waves.

That is a wonderful thing, just as it was wonderful for me to see one after another in a short space of time so many different varieties of animals, some on land, others on the water, and some in the air. Those that the earth sustains and shelters in its lodges are many; the Most High effortlessly providing them with nourishment, and with no need for anyone to care for them, giving them their natural instinct to protect themselves from their enemies. And some of them care so much about others that they take responsibility for their well-being, as does the unicorn,[110] which places its horn in the water to act as an antidote to the venom that poisonous insects secrete in it. And God gave them such true instincts that before drinking, the other animals wait for this medicine given by the unicorn, about which they all know.

The lions revealed their strength, and just as much do tigers, bears, ounces, wild boars, and rhinoceri. Others are not as fierce: elephants, deer, camels, each province and place having different sorts of animals. I shall finish this list of them with one that is most remarkable and so particularly caught my attention. It is much bigger than a large ox, brown, with a large head, and has a pouch on its chest that nature gives it to use when its young are born, carrying them there and using it as a luxurious litter. Its love is so great that it carries them with it until they are out of danger and can take care of themselves. As soon as they are born, it cleans and licks them and has them get into this pouch, where it feeds them, its milk not going dry until it is time to take them out; it keeps growing with the young so as not to squeeze them. Blessed be the providence and the wonders of the Most High.

There is another very big animal called a crocodile. It lives near the Nile River and feeds itself by tearing apart and eating animals. Its upper teeth are very sharp and the lower ones widely separated, and the two sets fit into each other. When it eats, the food gets in between its teeth, causing a lot of pain and suffering. When it finds itself in this distress, it opens its mouth wide to the air. And the Most High created a little bird called a *matroquillo*[111] that removes what is between the crocodile's teeth, living on just that. When the teeth are clean, the crocodile shakes its head to scare it away. I will not write more on the subject to keep it from becoming tiresome.

Oh, astonishing God and Lord and magnificent King! I do not know if I am more astonished that Your Highness created the *matroquillo* to clean the crocodile's teeth, or at the providence this shows, or that this cruel animal that lives on others should be so grateful as not only not to kill it, but also to signal its goodwill by letting it know it should leave.

Oh, uncreated God! How astonishing is your name as revealed by the wide world and the animals that live on its face, and how worthy You are, Lord, to be praised. What should cause mankind shame is that an animal appreciates the kindness done him by another, but people do not, my God, for the countless favors they receive from your generous hand. And who can count all that she receives? Impossible, for You created such diverse animals, each with its own purpose and reason, and Your Highness can do nothing in vain.

My Lord, looking into your divine mind and providence, what

grand design (supposing that Your Highness were obliged to formulate plans), what beneficent will, compels your magnificence to accomplish so many actions, to create so many animals and plants and grasses and lodges on the earth where all may take shelter and none lack for a place to retire in repose? May You be eternally blessed, uncreated Lord, for your countless wonders and acts of love.

Chapter 12

About the second element, water: its place and other properties and aspects of its nature.

Water is naturally cold and moist, heavier than air but not as heavy as earth, so for this reason its place is on and spreading over the surface of the globe. All the earth was covered with water, and it was necessary for the Most High to command that it withdraw to one part and place so that the earth might emerge and appear and become fruitful, providing a place for the grass, trees, and plants that sustain both mankind and the flying and earthbound animals.

The original body of water split into two when the Lord said, "Let there be a firmament in the midst of the waters; let the water under the firmament be separated from the water over the firmament." With these words God divided the waters into two parts. One rose up so high it went beyond the firmament, even above the sun, there freezing and becoming crystalline. I shall explain more about this water or heaven when it is time to talk about the heavenly spheres.

The other part of the water is at the lowest level, which is the surface of the earth. This is the place and location of the water that makes up the sea; the water from all the rivers and fountains, being so slippery, insistently runs to the sea, its natural place and the lowest point; for just as the earth is naturally round, so is water, finding no rest or repose until it reaches its home. And it was necessary for the Maker Himself to place limits on the waters. With his word and powerful arm, He commanded them not to rise above the line that marks their boundaries, for His Highness has set the point beyond which they should not go.

And what His Immense Majesty commanded was important, for since of its own nature water is so flexible, without difficulty moving and taking itself from one place to another, it could easily (and painfully for us mortals) once again cover the earth and embrace it all, as it did when it was first created, and then we would suffer the flood many more times, the waters covering the earth all the way up to the highest and most lofty mountains, as happened when Noah took refuge with all his family in the ark. On that occasion, the water rose fifteen (and I am not sure it was not more) cubits higher than the highest mountain. This danger might well threaten us were we not free of it by the command and providence of the Highest, the magnificent Lord, for even the most violent elements obey Him as their Creator, and none offer Him resistance, except for a cruel and ungrateful mankind, for we are the ones who receive the benefits derived from the obedience of the elements and God's command over them.

Water is highly instrumental and more powerful than the other elements. It embraces the earth, taking possession of it, rising by the sun's energy into the high and lofty air, there causing rain, dew, snow, hail, and fog. Finally, its natural power mitigates and even neutralizes that of fire, overcoming it in spite of that being such a strong and all-consuming element.

Water is very important, the main resource necessary for our natural life. It all goes to the sea, into which run all the rivers and fountains, though they later spring forth again, spreading their waters over the earth to be of help to the needy in all that they lack. Through this wonderful arrangement and providence, God directs the various rivers, distributing them without any effort on the part of mankind.

The sea is an astonishing creature, and no less so the multitude and variety of fish it contains. The reason seawater is salty I perceived and understood to be that the energy of the sun's rays raises the finest particles of water and leaves behind the heavier and most earthbound ones. And although this might by natural means be part of the reason why the water is salty, the fact is that the Most High, making use of this natural cause, adds a lot of his own providence and plan. In the first place, His Highness created those salty and bitter waters because they were more suited to and effective for preserving such an infinity of fish as live in them, for seawater prevents their spoiling or rotting. And in addition to being healthy for fish, they are better for ships since they are denser.

The sea is called the beginning and end of the waters, for they all (as has been said) are born from and return to it. And although it is true that many thousands of rivers and fountains flow into it, that does not cause it to grow. The reason is that the sea, while it is the repository of all the waters, also has many vents through which it gives off as much water as it receives.

Rivers are produced and caused by a flowing together of many fountains, and when they rise, so too the rivers they feed. Fountains are caused by the water that runs through the veins of the earth and its hollows, sometimes finding their way blocked and being unable to turn back due to the pressure of the colliding waters, likewise unable to move to the side or down due to the density and thickness of the rock, and so necessarily rising, thereby producing springs.

But one can also observe a wonder of the Most High in the fact that although the rivers and fountains are caused by the sea, for in it they have their beginning and origin, still they are not salty as it is. I noticed this contradiction but was shown that it happens naturally, something the Maker of all things makes use of and directs according to the purposes of his most high[112] providence, which is that the waters should become sweet for the natural well-being of mankind. If this magnificent King did not so direct through his providence, the salt water would be extremely harmful. The natural cause and means that His Highness takes for such an important thing is this: just as living creatures take on the properties of the region through which they are passing, losing those they had at the beginning and acquiring other very different ones—as we see in the example given by summer, when it is hot and the air becomes hot, too, while cold in the winter—just so the waters of the rivers and fountains, going through different and diverse lands, slowly lose that bitter acidity they bring from the sea, taking on instead a smooth sweetness. This is the providence of the Most High; it is good for all, as it is a great good for the sea that its waters are salty. When I saw this creature, I truly perceived its Creator within it.

The sea is bigger than the land. The beauty it shows is great. And I thought to myself, if the water all went away or it were possible for it to dry up, what a big empty space would be left! God left that there for the water, making it to its measure in the beginning when He created the heavens and the earth. This big hole now filled by the sea is wonderful to see, with all the hollows where the fish are. There are craggy rocks and as the result of shipwrecks, the sea holds accumulated treasures.

The extent and circumference of this creature is something to see; to the unaided eye it appears to have no end, such is its breadth. There is a large quantity of fish for the delight and use of mankind: whales, for example, which are as big as large rooms, and all the parts of their bodies can be put to excellent use. So many salmon, bass, lobsters, tuna, and many other large and small fish, and all of them know to move through the sea, picking out their own lodges and places to live. Then there are the ways and means they use to flee and protect themselves from each other, although sometimes it does not save them for the small become the food of the big ones, some the graves of others. Yet this does not happen without being the providence of the Most High, for it is his will to permit and command that of the many small fish, some more than others should fall victims to these trials and death. And even among those that fall into the hands of fishermen, the Lord picks out some more than others according to his will.

Oh, astonishing and magnificent King, how your power shines resplendent in this marvelous element of water! My Lord and husband, with your remarkable providence You made this creature so pure, its bright and clear body. And not only did Your Highness, my King, create it but also ordered and took action so that it be salty, as was needful, and the rivers, by your providence, sweet. Oh, Author and Lord of the universe! With the strength of your arm You ordained not only that this element be enclosed within the sea but also, so that it might not cost mankind so dear to look for water to meet our needs, You sent a stream to every province and corner of the earth so that all might satisfy their thirst and enjoy fully such a beautiful creature. Oh, how great and powerful You are, my God, and especially for holding back the wild waves of the sea stirred up when the weather changes!

If Your Highness did not do so, the world would drown—that happening to us not only from the extreme turbulence of the terrible winds and storms that often happen at sea but also from the very high bulges and swellings in it often caused by the moon. For if at the time of the flood all the tall and lofty peaks were covered and the water rose much higher than they, how would we avoid drowning now if your providence did not come to our aid?

Blessed be such a Lord, so well obeyed by his creatures. In this your Majesty shows Himself to be the true God. I ask the pagans whether by any chance the gods of metal and wood they worship would be powerful enough to do this wonder. Would the water obey them? Would they create the smallest fish or sustain it? No, indeed. My Lord, Your Highness alone is the Creator of the heavens and the earth and the elements, God of Abraham, Isaac, and Jacob, and it is You who sustains and gives life to them all. May You be eternally blessed and recognized as a magnificent and generous Lord worthy of honor and glory. Amen.

Chapter 13

About the third element, air, and its particular properties and place.

I t is unquestionably true that the element air exists, for we experience it with our sense of touch even if we do not with that of sight. It is divided into three regions—high, low, and middle— all different in their properties.

The highest is hot and dry through the circumstance of being next to the element fire. I encountered it when I was flying through the air on my way to learning about the kind deeds the Most High did for me. In this high region, comets are generated. The second one, situated between the other two, is very cold because it does not participate in the fire above it or receive, at least as much as the first does, the reflection of the sun's rays from below. The third and lowest region has those properties naturally associated with air, although it takes them on according to the circumstances; it is hot when the sun

shines upon it, moist from the proximity of water, and cold when
the weather is. In this region, the third, are generated fog, dew,
and frost.

There are many sorts of winds that are not really air but are produced by the breathing out of the earth; they have various properties
and effects, though it does not seem appropriate to explain them
here. The element air, though, is very important and instrumental in
producing some things and sustaining others.

In all things is the Lord marvelous, nor did He create idly or by
chance but with great wisdom. There are many birds that soar
through the air, parting it with their flight, a reason for the Most
High to be praised. In one of the properties of eagles,[113] there is a
strong reason for such praise (just as it gave me a very big one to recognize the magnificence of this King), and it is that when they want
to take their little ones out to fly and so have them begin to take care
of themselves, they take them up to the loftiest part of their flight.
Then, in order to test them—and this is something I observed—they
place them looking directly into the sun's rays, and if they are stunned
and cannot bear it, they deny that they are their children and drop
them. This mystery of nature strikes me as a very appropriate parable
for parents, for God gave them children to bring up with the care they
should have, educating them and not allowing any love of flesh and
blood to lead them to fail to admonish and punish their children
when in their actions they do not look to God eternal who sustains
them, even though this may mean the parents, in their desire that
their children serve the Most High, seem to deny the love they naturally have for them; they should be parents who want eternal life for
them, not the life that perishes.

Cranes also have a remarkable property[114] showing great concern
for each other, for while some sleep, others are sentries standing
guard. To do this better, they have a stone held in their hand or claw;
it helps them stay awake because they awaken if it falls, and so they
can warn the others of dangers that may threaten them from other
animals. What a warning this is for churchmen, into whose care God
entrusted souls! Notice that they should all be awake even though
their flock sleeps. And they should not feel this is a burden, for all of

us, even though we have no one except ourselves to answer for, need to keep watch and be vigilant against the enemies who constantly hem us in. And how much more those who have so many to answer for! Remember that it is wrong for a guard of Israel to sleep or doze. The Israel of the Most High God and Lord is the soul, and it is guarded by prelates, who are the watchmen over their flocks. The stone they should have in their hands following the example of the crane is Christ Our Lord, who is a model to awaken them when they see the vigilance of that careful shepherd, though it may also represent an absence of comforts and luxuries, a measure that will keep churchmen from sleep and lead them to feel concern for the needs of their flocks.

There are many beautiful birds. The heron is exceptionally so, as are parrots, hawks, goshawks, and countless more, for some delight us with their songs, others please by their appearance, letting us see the variety of colors beautifying the feathers in which their Creator dressed them. It is something pleasing to contemplate. In fact, all the birds are, and give cause to praise their Lord. I will not list them because it would be tiresome to do so, including their properties and habits, though all that is for mankind's delight.

Oh, Author of all things created, Lord God of Israel, how wonderful You are in your works! Wonderful for having given us travelers here below the element air, so pretty and having such a tenuous body that it does not keep us from seeing the structure and grandeur of the heavens, for in seeing them we may remember the great King and his court, and the happy reward of enjoying You in the heavenly Jerusalem. Then we, poor pilgrims beholding our homeland, take heart and find new energy to do all those things of which we are capable through He who comforts us. May You be blessed, my Lord, for You created such a diversity of beautiful birds so that we human creatures might imitate them and correct our negligence in something so important as is serving your Majesty; You created birds for the support, delight, pleasure, and luxury of mankind, so that with their harmonious music rolling out of their beaks as though from harps, they might entertain and delight the ears of all creatures and lead us to praise their Maker and Creator. And true it is, my Lord, that they compel us to do so.

Even though I am dust and ashes, I do and shall offer that praise forever, as long as my life may last; should I not, let it come to an end. Should I not love and praise You, that would be not life, but death. May it please Your Highness that I die to all things imperfect and live to all things good, and God in me, for He is the life in which I live and for which I die.

Chapter 12[115]

About the fourth element, fire; in which its existence is proved, something I myself saw, and where it is.

Elemental fire has its own natural home above the third region of the air, for it is more rarefied and diffuse than the other elements and rises above them; although invisible, it is there, for at the time I was experiencing this mystical knowledge of all things in the way I have said—an angel staying in my place while I went to see these marvels—with that opportunity I touched the region of fire with my hands. I say with my hands because I could feel how it was. And although it is true that by its nature elemental fire is all-consuming and scorching, there is no substance in its sphere to feed it, nor can there be, nor is it necessary, for an element (when it is in its own natural home) has no need of any other substance to preserve it, and although we do not see it, still it exists. The reason we do not is that it is not visible the way something material is. It cannot burst into flame or burn, being so pure, simple, and rarefied, and, indeed, it is all that.

Water is ten times more diffuse than earth, air ten times more than water, fire ten times more than air. Fire is naturally hot and dry, its heat greater than that of air and its dryness that of earth. This element warms but does not burn, as I experienced. I mean it does not consume things. Its way of heating is through a big slow heat like that given by the sun in the east. It is a pretty element, and the Lord exalted his work.

May You be praised, Lord, for these many marvels, for having created such a pretty creature and sustaining it naturally without the need for any other substance, and without its ever being used up. This creature pleases me by its activity, and would that all creatures had the same, especially we rational ones, so that we might serve and love Your Highness for these magnificent things, for your high wisdom hates the lukewarm, and they provoke in You a strong dislike.

Give me, my King, even though I might not deserve it nor be qualified for it, the light and fire of the Holy Spirit to love and serve You. And should all that I have on my conscience be an obstacle, You have the power to grant me the right inclination, the spiritual quality and light for perfect love, and the fire and fruition of the High Spirit so that they may purify my soul, just as physical fire did Isaiah's. So be it. Amen.

Chapter 15

About the heavenly region and some mysteries regarding it that were shown to me, and about the first heaven and its planet, the moon.

Through his kindness and compassion, the Lord showed me the heavenly region the same way He did the other things and said to me, "My wife and turtledove, pay attention to all this and offer the praises owed me by my human creatures, for they have forgotten the kind favors I did for their benefit, and give me the payment that from ingratitude the other mortals do not." No sooner had He said this to me than my holy guardian angels carried me away, my principal guardian angel staying in my place, while the other five who care for me accompanied and moved with me in the same manner by which I went to see the other things that I came to know in these assumptions, which by the grace of the Most High I was able to experience. I went up into the heavens and personally witnessed and clearly saw all that follows.

There are ten heavens that are in continual movement, eleven in all. The last and highest is the empyrean heaven, which is subject to no motion, being the place of quiet and repose where lives the great and magnificent King as well as the blessed chosen by His Highness. This is the celestial Jerusalem, the heavenly home. I shall talk about it at the end.

[First Heaven][116]

The first heaven, the one closest to us, is the sphere we see as very beautiful and pleasant to look at. It is separated from the earth, on its concave surface, by 6,247 leagues. In this sphere is located the moon, whose body has a circumference of 1,663 leagues; if the moon were in the eighth heaven instead of the first, we would not be able to see it since it is smaller than the stars. Its sphere or heaven contains 756,758 leagues, and the thickness of the crystal is 118,878 leagues. The moon moves from east to west at 31,532 leagues per hour. The body of the moon appeared to me with a resplendent brightness, like something white and dense, cold and damp, though it is hot to some degree by virtue of the warmth it receives from the sun.

The sphere's body is also glassy, white but tending toward a diaphanous light blue. As I penetrated, it felt like a beautiful cloud; the touch on the skin was soft, gentle, and pleasant. It is extremely beautiful, especially when seen so close. In going through it at high speed, I covered a certain time and distance, though I did not go so fast that I failed to see and learn about this heavenly body. Its grace and beauty were remarkable.

Oh, wonderful and magnificent God! Who is not amazed to see your providence in the fact that this heaven remains always in view as a pretty sight for us travelers here below and that You are so prodigal in your generosity, my Most High Lord, that the moon is visible to the world at night both to us and in other parts of the globe, and it lights up the night for the Perioecians, the Antoecians, the Antipodes, and all the others? And Your Highness directed the moon to travel a set distance from east to west in an hour, and that amount was so precisely and correctly set when Your Majesty created the body of the moon that it has never had to speed up nor failed to move, while mankind, created to love You, does not. What is to be seen here, my King, except your word and command? How faithful is your watchful care and how well, Most High Lord, this creature obeys You. By all your creatures may You be praised, Lord of all the universe. Amen.

Second Heaven

The second heaven, on its concave surface, is separated from the face of the earth by 7,901,917 leagues. Its circumference is 521,159,700 leagues.

The body of this second heaven is more beautiful than the first, for the closer they approach the empyrean, the more they reflect the spirit in brightness and beauty. In this heaven, there is a star or planet called Mercury. Its circumference is a hundred paces. This star travels from east to west in an hour the distance of 801,620 leagues. The properties of this star are mixed, hot, cold, and moist.

Third Heaven

The third heaven, on its concave surface, is separated from the earth by 86,858,699 leagues. Its thickness is 235,678,750 leagues. Its circumference is 1,935,232,200 leagues.

This third heaven is larger than the first two because it encloses them, and the closer they come to the last ones, the bigger, more beautiful, and brighter they become. In this heaven, there is a star or planet called Venus. It is the morning star. Its breadth is 175 leagues.

Fourth Heaven

The fourth heaven, on its concave surface, is separated from the earth by 322,037,449 leagues. Its thickness is 657,985,670 leagues. Its circumference is 5,883,146,220 leagues.

In this fourth heaven, there is just one planet, the sun. It is in the middle position among the planets as king and lord over them, giving its light and brilliance to the heavens, stars, and all the earth. The sun's breadth is 5950 leagues. This beautiful planet is hot and dry in moderation, and this is the reason all the earth's plants and fruits grow and ripen.

Fifth Heaven

The fifth heaven, on its concave surface, is separated from the earth by 980,593,119 leagues. Its thickness and depth is 985,678,787 leagues. Its circumference is 11,797,218,942 leagues.

In this heaven is the planet Mars. It is extremely beautiful and brilliant due to the light it receives from the sun. Its circumference is 240 leagues.

Sixth Heaven

The sixth heaven is extremely beautiful and delightful by virtue of all it receives from the sun and the empyrean heaven. On its concave surface, it is separated from the earth by 1,966,201,906 leagues. Its thickness is 6,578,917,718 leagues. Its circumference is 51,270,724,590 leagues.

In this heaven is the planet Jupiter, whose body is ninety-four times bigger than the earth. This planet is naturally hot and moist and favorable to the earth.

Seventh Heaven

The seventh heaven is pretty, bright, and beautiful. On its concave surface, it is separated from the earth by 8,505,119,514 leagues. Its depth and thickness is 7,650,976,500 leagues. Its circumference is 97,176,583,590 leagues.

In this seventh heaven is Saturn, whose body is one hundred times larger than the whole earth. This star is naturally cold and dry.

Eighth Heaven

The eighth heaven is exceedingly beautiful and adorned with such a multitude of stars that it exceeds all the others in brightness, being next to the empyrean; moreover, it has the luminosity of the stars and the light it receives from the sun. On its concave surface, it is separated from the earth by 16,196,960,014 leagues. Its depth and thickness is 89,765,890,060 leagues. Its circumference is 635,721,318,190 leagues.

In this eighth heaven are set the stars as we see them from here below; they are all there except the seven planets already mentioned. The whole heaven revolves very rapidly from east to west as the others do. Of all the stars that fill this heaven, there are twenty-two that are the biggest and best known. Fifteen are of first magnitude. Each of these fifteen is a hundred times larger than the earth. Forty-five are of second magnitude, smaller than the first fifteen, but eighty-nine times larger than the earth. There are 208 third-magnitude stars, smaller than the ones described so far, but each one seventy times larger than the earth. There are 474 of fourth magnitude and size; they are smaller than the ones described so far, but each one is fifty-three times larger than the earth. There are 217 fifth-magnitude stars, but each one is thirty-five times larger than the earth. There are sixty-three smaller than any mentioned yet, but each one is seventeen times larger than the earth. And finally, all the stars, no matter how small, are larger than the earth. Only God is able to count them. The body of these stars is like polished silver, only transparently clear.

Ninth Heaven

The ninth heaven is exceedingly beautiful, but in it there are no stars or planets. Its beauty is greater than that of the purest crystal. This and the following heaven are called aqueous. God created them from the waters that he commanded to rise above the firmament; he purified and made them beautiful, then froze them. These two heavens were created by God as protection from the radiance of the empyrean heaven that beats upon them. How beautiful!

On its concave surface, it is separated from the earth by 105,961,885,074 leagues. Its thickness is 299,824,574,900 leagues. Its circumference is 2,434,012,731,350 leagues.

Tenth Heaven

The tenth heaven, like the preceding one, is called aqueous. It is the prime mover because with its movement it pulls along with it all the lower spheres. It is larger than all the others because it embraces and surrounds them. On its concave surface, it is separated from the earth by 405,785,453,974 leagues. Its thickness and depth is

9,872,387,657,802 leagues. Its circumference is 61,669,308,678,162 leagues.

The circumference on the concave surface of all the ten heavens has been stated. Likewise what it is on the upper surface, for as the highest level borders only on infinite space, all the dimensions can be calculated from what has been stated. And since the tenth heaven touches the empyrean, I will say how far it is from the earth so that the number of leagues may be known from the sphere and face of the earth up to the empyrean heaven, which is next to the tenth heaven. To figure that out, I have added in the air up to the first heaven and the thicknesses of the ten heavens. Adding it all up, the result is 10,278,173,111,766 leagues. That is the distance that separates us on the surface of the earth from the sphere of the brightly shining empyrean heaven. May the Lord give us his grace that we not be unworthy to go there. Amen.

4

Mystical Journey

or Sor María, the first three years of life in the convent were terribly trying.[1] She suffered physically from almost constant illnesses, and spiritually from an inner life full of what she considered diabolical temptations, including some very persistent sexual ones, and an exaggerated idea of her own sinfulness. This scrupulosity, which her autobiography indicates is a continuation of her negative self-image as a child, caused her to impose painful and inappropriate forms of penitence on herself. These acts of penitence were followed by comforting "*exterioridades*"—trances, visions, and even levitations—either a gift from Heaven, as Sor María believed, or the product of psychological and physiological tensions she felt from her supposed sins and her efforts to purge them. When the exterioridades took place, the young nun, kneeling and absorbed in prayer, lost consciousness, swayed from side to side, and grew deadly pale, seeming to those present to lose contact with the ground.

In this state, it was not hard to take the step from the deeply rooted and intimate concerns expressed in *Face of the Earth* to the experience of bilocation. As Sor María described the experience, God already had shown her all of the universe, but now He was giving her more specific and detailed information about the lands to the north of Mexico. She was convinced that on hundreds of occasions she was carried there through the air and felt the drastic changes in temperature and saw from above the terrestrial globe divided into day and night. She always preached to the Indians, and more than once in pagan lands she won the crown of martyrdom for which she, like Teresa de Avila and Kempe, longed.

Much later in her life, Sor María wrote that at the end of the three years, after having with all her heart begged God to stop sending these favors, the trances ceased. In spite of that statement, the period of time involved, three years or several more, is not entirely clear. But however long the bilocations lasted, she naturally had told her confessor about them. He was an older priest who shared with the nuns in Sor María's convent a keen enthusiasm for extravagantly marvelous cases in religious life, phenomena not at all uncommon among Spanish mystics of the time. "Not a cautious man," as Sor María would describe him years later, he spread the good news within the order, generating an interest that eventually resulted in a letter to Alonso de Benavides, director of the Franciscan missions in New Mexico, requesting him to investigate whether or not the Indians knew anything about the nun.

What happened as a consequence of that request was narrated by Benavides in two reports, one to the king in 1630, and an expanded version in 1634 to the Pope. The impact of these reports, which were widely read at court, translated into several languages, and responsible for Felipe IV meeting Sor María, was reinforced by a letter the director sent to the missionaries in New Mexico after he returned to Spain. That letter summarized—very much from his own point of view, as we shall see—a long official interview that he conducted with Sor María in Agreda. Thus Benavides' accounts, more than Sor María's, are the direct sources of the legend that, thanks to Franciscan teaching, has survived in New Mexico and Texas.

Sor María's own interpretation of her experiences was very different. The Inquisition, set in motion on her case in 1635 and again in 1649 by the nun's supposed participation in a political plot tied to her friendship with the king,[2] examined her about the bilocation. She first gave oral testimony to the inquisitors who interrogated her, and then sent a written account to Pedro Manero, minister general of the order in Spain.

From any perspective, it is a fascinating story, so I will let Benavides and Sor María tell it in their own words. Just a few observations may set the stage in greater detail. Although Benavides had chosen to wear

the habit of a friar minor, he had not given up an energetic and enter-
prising character. The Spanish crown was covering the costs of Franciscan missionary work, and the 1630 report stressed the benefits, both
practical and otherworldly, of the order's presence on the northern border of New Spain. On returning to Spain to argue for the missionary
cause with the greater insistence made possible by being at court, Benavides had as an only partially hidden agenda, aside from a budgetary
increase, the goal of creating a new diocese of New Mexico and being
appointed its first bishop. The diocese did not fall to his lot, but Benavides did manage to become a bishop, though in the other Indies, in
Asia, and he apparently died on the journey there.[3]

In detailing his achievements administering the spiritual life of New
Mexico, Benavides would not have objected to a miracle such as Sor
María's bilocation that showed heavenly satisfaction and even active
cooperation in taking the Gospel to the region. What is more, a miracle
that included teaching the basics of the catechism to the natives prior
to the arrival of the missionaries would have helped the order defend
itself from criticism, which in fact it was subjected to, that it was baptizing en masse without having communicated the essential concepts
of the new faith.[4] Kendrick, who along with Pérez Villanueva and
Kessell has advocated a rationalistic yet serious historiographical approach to the bilocation, suggests that when Benavides received the
initial letter of inquiry about Sor María, he saw his opportunity and
knew how to make the most of it, asking informants in the Jumano
tribe leading questions that encouraged them to give the answers he
wanted.

There are perfectly plausible reasons why the Indians might have
known how to give Benavides the desired answers—and why they
would have wanted to do so. In their annual trip to the region recently
settled by the Spanish, the Jumanos would have learned something of
Catholicism and seen images of the Virgin Mary dressed in blue, a
starting point for their statement that the same color was worn by the
lady who urged them to invite the Franciscans to their lands in West
Texas so they might be baptized. In fact, for several years, they had
been asking that missionaries be sent to them. Kendrick argues they
probably had other motives for saying what Benavides wanted to hear—
trade, protection, and curiosity, for example—a circumstance that

would address the disconcerting detail that never before had they mentioned the lady in blue who repeatedly came down from the sky. Kendrick proposes a parallel with the case of the Indian called El Turco, who led the Coronado expedition from New Mexico to Kansas with stories, described by the English historian as "lies," about a people whose features were much more grandly mythological than those found among the Wichita Indians at the end of the journey.

There is no conclusive proof for this interpretation of the bilocation, just as there is none on the other side of the question. All we have is what Benavides wrote, what the Southwest Indians told explorers, and Sor María's own account of her experience and the interview. Still, if one does not automatically reject the possibility of a bilocation, the detour around the extant documents seems much smaller. What we can add today, twenty years after Kendrick's study, is a growing recognition by scholars studying Spain's first exploration of America that frequently the participants, Europeans as much as the indigenous peoples, let themselves be caught up in and guided by a fusion of practical material interests and archetypal elements of myth—taken from one culture but adapted to the other to meet the needs of the circumstances. If we were to apply that approach to the bilocation, we would talk not about lies but about the powerful role of the imagination in both Benavides' and the Jumanos' reaction to the news of what the nun had told her confessor, and in Sor María, too, for she participated vicariously but effectively in the exploration of the Southwest.[5]

The report to Manero reveals another, almost anti-mystical side of Sor María. She has matured, unquestionably, but one cannot ignore that she was writing immediately upon emerging from the shadow of the Inquisition. She needed to refute Benavides' letter, and she knew how to distance herself from practically all of his sensational assertions. It does not seem overbold to suppose, in spite of what she told her superiors years later, that in the famous interview she let herself be swayed a little by the insistent New Mexican director, and that the neutral truth of how she understood the bilocation lay between two more personal truths: what she felt in the excited enthusiasm of 1631, and the cooler moment of circumspect reflection under the threat of the Inquisition.

What is beyond any doubt is Sor María's skill as a literary self-defender. Not wasting a scrap of the advantage of having the last word against her dead opponent, Sor María convinces us, as she convinced Manero, that she is sincere when she affirms she had always distrusted the authenticity of this famed mystical experience. She proposes a more sensible interpretation that looks for acceptable explanations. Then, with impeccable logic, she proposes the probable origin of what we come to believe were surely just foolish misunderstandings and exaggerations based on rumor. She convincingly identifies mitigating circumstances: her nervousness as a young woman in the authority-laden, threatening presence of several "graves padres" of her order, the involuntary nature of her experience, the intense suffering that accompanied it, and her heroic but failed efforts to prevent others from generating painful publicity.

At both the beginning and the end of the letter, Sor María wields the checkmate argument, picked up in the manuscript and stressed by Kendrick: she asserts her "trips" lasted only until 1623, while Benavides and the Indians maintained (as she herself did in a letter she wrote and gave to Benavides to send to the missionaries) that they were still going on in 1631. Her protestations notwithstanding, there is no statement by Sor María contradicting Benavides, nor any other document dating from 1623 to 1650, that supports her later declarations that the bilocations ended earlier and that Benavides wrote and placed in her hands her much-reprinted letter of 1631 to the missionaries in New Mexico.[6] Kessell's 1992 study inclines toward accepting Sor María's later disavowal but leaves the question open. Readers will now be able to compare for themselves the tone and style of her two letters on the subject.

In Teresa de Avila's somewhat similar descriptions of amazing favors from God, she was forced into self-contradictions that reveal more about a nun's powerless situation with ecclesiastical fathers than what she truly meant or thought. In Weber's view, an adroit use of "concessions and qualifications" helped save her from condemnation by the Inquisition in her tightrope walk between orthodoxy and heresy.[7] Equally important may be the fact that the dominated party in a hierarchical confrontation often finds it necessary to acquiesce in word and—to make the surrender easier—at a certain level of thought revising her self-image in the interests of strategy and safety. When we are wrestling instead of dancing with society, what we think about ourselves changes as we instinctively move for protection.

Jean Franco has studied geographic flights of the spirit from a feminist perspective and believes they, like women's visions in general, are poor models because they represent only momentary escapes from hierarchical control. In this view, visions are harmful to women because they continue the stereotype of women as being irrational.[8] Arenal and Schlau, in contrast, regard visions more sympathetically and document repeated cases in which they contributed to women's self-confidence and social recognition.[9]

Franco has observed, however, that "this flight was the feminine equivalent of the heroic journey of self-transformation, with the difference that it met no obstacles and was less a narrative than an epiphany."[10] Sor María's *Face of the Earth* fits this characterization, but her account of the bilocation does not: she actively preaches, converts Indians, and repeatedly accepts death. With its heroic nature and a form modeled on the exploits of the male conquistadors and missionaries (from which she was excluded), Sor María's narrative seems closely related to the journey of self-transformation referred to by Franco.

In the Christian mythology familiar to Sor María, one such journey is the harrowing of hell, the Savior's descent into the underworld after his crucifixion to bring out the souls of the just who were born before his sacrifice. As in this Christian expression of the story, the narrative usually reflects a compassionate, altruistic motive: a desire to save primarily others and only secondarily oneself through confrontation with death. The saving and solitary work of Sor María in remote New Mexico, rewarded with martyrdom and return to life, reflect the symbols of heroism in her culture but defy their gender limitations because Sor María appropriates them for a woman—herself.[11]

The fact that mythical journeys often involve flight can be intuitively understood by recalling dreams in which freedom from the body's weight and movement combines with the sense of well-being produced by being in a high place, such as a watchtower or a peak, and enjoying both a wide view and a safe position. Being above means knowing and being able to do more than when one is below. For this reason, God is necessarily the Most High, the divine attribute that most attracted Sor María.

Like Sor María during her bilocation, shamans in many cultures remain in a trance while the soul travels to and then returns from the supernatural world. They think of themselves as birds coming from distant lands bringing valuable and powerful information to effect important change. Confronted as a teenager with permanent confinement brought about by her mother's resolve, Sor María used her imagination to look for a heroic solution beyond the convent walls. The fact that she spoke of being carried by angels also reflects the widespread symbol of flight as the means of access to spiritual power. Angels, the traditional winged messengers between Heaven and earth in the Judeo-Christian tradition, correspond to the shamans' birds.

But in view of contemporary Latin American fiction's magical realism, which incorporates much of traditional Hispanic mysticism, perhaps the time has come to argue again the other side of the question. The church has long held a belief in the possibility of corporeal bilocation: saints said to have enjoyed this gift include Anthony of Padua, Catherine of Ricci, and Philip Neri. Closer to Sor María's explanation—that an angel in her form intervened for her—are medieval legends. In the thirteenth-century Cantigas de Santa María, the Virgin Mary assumes the appearance of an unhappy nun and takes her place so that the sister may leave for adventures on the outside, one of which involves eloping with her knight.

In this century, related beliefs center on the possibility of mental, not physical, bilocation. A Jesuit investigator of saints whose biographies include parapsychological aspects concluded that "the telepathic visualizing of conditions at a distance does not seem to involve of necessity any preternatural agency."[12] "Out-of-body experiences" are now studied regularly, and close brushes with death, certain drugs, and even some learnable techniques reportedly precipitate them. Nor are they limited to seeing one's own body from an outside perspective; many include travel over considerable distances, travel whose "reality" appears to be confirmed by information acquired in the places visited and sightings of the ethereal body by witnesses and instruments. Among such case studies, Sor María de Agreda's bilocation is not atypical.[13]

Manuscripts of the Report to Father Manero

The two reports by Benavides and his letter written after the interview with Sor María have been published several times; there are even English translations, from one of which the passages incorporated into this chapter are taken.[14] The report to Manero, in spite of its value as a biographical source, has not been published previously, although Serrano y Sanz did publish a short passage near the beginning of this century.[15] The National Library in Madrid has four copies.[16] The one edited here (MS 153) has the following note at the end: "Here concludes the sixth treatise of the fragments by the Venerable Mother María de Jesús; this copy of it was finished on the day of San Juan Capistrano, the twenty-third day of the month of October, Convent of Our Lady of Hope in Ocaña, a community in this holy province of Castile of the regular observance of St. Francis." I have designated this manuscript with the letter O, for Ocaña. I have reproduced the original numbering of the paragraphs, about which there is a note on the ninth folio: "Which goes by paragraphs, just as I found it in the little notebooks." The fact that the first paragraph is numbered 228 is due to the placement of the work within a compilation of others by Sor María, where it appears as the fifth treatise.

The text of O shows few signs of garbling or of likely divergences from the original meaning. Nonetheless, in six places I chose to clarify it by comparison with another manuscript. The one used, MS 7618, although copied a century later, has a voucher for its reliability. The following note appears on its last folio:

> It agrees with the version from which it was copied and which was given to me for that purpose by Doctor Don Juan María de Rodezno, member of His Majesty's Council on the Holy General Inquisition, to whom I returned it and to whom inquiries may be directed. Madrid, July 6, 1678, and I, the secretary Don Domingo de la Cantolla Miera, have signed it. What is copied on these 28 folios is found in a quarto notebook containing 49 unnumbered manuscript pages.
>
> This copy agrees with the one described immediately above and has

been sent to His Majesty in compliance with his royal order of September 26 to direct it to Rome, the order on whose authority I act, and I have signed on November 20 in the year 1769. Manuel de Argumosa, Secretary of the Council.

I refer to this copy with the letter R, for Rodezno. Its division into paragraphs and their numbering are distinct from those in O.

From Benavides' 1634 Report

Setting out eastward from the villa of Santa Fe, center of New Mexico, and traveling through more than one hundred leagues of country belonging to the Apaches Vaqueros mentioned in the preceding chapter, one reaches the Xumana nation, whose conversion was miraculous. Several years earlier, messengers came from this nation every summer to beg Father fray Juan de Salas, in particular, that he go to baptize them, as they wanted to become Christians. They had become attached to him on seeing him come to the rescue of some unfortunate people that they were ill-treating. For lack of friars, we did not send anyone to preach to them, nor did they inform us who had advised them to do this, nor did we ask, convinced that they acted like many other nations who had also asked for baptism, after hearing the truth of our holy Catholic faith. Finally, in the year 1629, when more than four years had passed since we had had any news from Spain, there arrived in New Mexico the thirty friars sent to us at that time by the Catholic king. These friars told us from an account which had been given them the previous year by the archbishop of Mexico, that it was common news in Spain that a nun named María de Jesús de la Concepción, of the Discalced order of Saint Francis, residing in the town of Agreda in the province of Burgos, was miraculously transported to New Mexico to preach our holy Catholic faith to those savage Indians. The archbishop had charged these same friars to inquire into this affair and had informed them of the report he had brought to the Indies from Spain two years before. He added that it had been given to him by a reliable person who assured him that it happened in the following manner:

It is very probable that in the continued exploration of New Mexico and the conversion of those souls, a kingdom called Tidan will soon be reached, four hundred leagues beyond Mexico to the west, or between west and north, which, as far as is known, is situated between New Mexico and Quivira. If by chance the cosmography should be erroneous, it would be helpful to take note of three other kingdoms, called Chillescas, Guismanes, and Aburcos, respectively, which border on the said kingdom of Tidan. When these have been explored, we will endeavor to learn whether there is any knowledge of our holy Catholic faith in them, and by what manner and means our Lord made it known to them. In authorizing this inquiry, the archbishop says: "We, Don Francisco Manzo y Zúñiga, archbishop elect of Mexico, member of the council of his Majesty and of the royal Council of the Indies, do hereby urgently recommend this inquiry to the reverend custodian and fathers of the said conversion in order that they may carry it out with the solicitude, faith, and devotion that the case demands, and that they duly inform us concerning its results, so that they may be verified in legal form. This will no doubt redound in great spiritual and temporal advancement to the glory and service of our Lord. Issued in Mexico on May 18, 1628."

When this news reached New Mexico in 1629, we were in complete ignorance of it, nor had we ever heard of Mother María de Jesús. But we soon noticed that the great care and solicitude with which the Xumana Indians came to us every summer to plead for friars to go and baptize them must have been through inspiration from heaven. When this news arrived, they had already come a few days earlier to make the same request, and they were lodged in the pueblo. We called them to the convent and asked them their motive in coming every year to ask for baptism with such insistency. Gazing at a portrait of Mother Luisa in the convent, they said: "A woman in similar garb wanders among us over there, always preaching, but her face is not old like this, but young." Asked why they had not told us before, they answered, "Because you did not ask us, and we thought she was around here too." These Indians repeated this same story in different localities without variation or difference in their accounts.

Immediately we decided to send the said Father fray Juan de Salas and fray Diego López, his companion, both theologians and priests of great zeal. With these same Indians as guides, they departed on that apostolic mission. After traveling more than one hundred leagues, crossing the country of the Apache Vaqueros toward the east, they reached the Xumana nation, who came out to receive them in procession, carrying a large cross and garlands of flowers. They learned from the Indians that the same nun had instructed them as to how they should come out in procession to receive them, and she had helped them to decorate the cross. A very large number of people stopped in that place and asked for baptism with loud cries. The Indian women with suckling babes seized their little arms and lifted them on high, shouting also for baptism for them since they were incapable of asking for it themselves.

After working there for several days in catechizing them, and having set up a large cross where they always gathered to pray, these friars decided to come back to us to get more workers, as the harvest was great. Taking leave of the Indians, they charged them to worship the holy cross and to have faith that in it they would find satisfaction for all their needs. The chief captain said: "Father, we are as yet of no value before God, because we are not baptized; we are like the beasts in the fields. You are a priest of God and can do much with that holy cross; heal our many sick before you depart." They brought people with all kinds of infirmities, and when these two friars made the sign of the cross over them and recited the gospel of Saint Luke, *Loquente Jesu* and the prayer of our Lady, *Concédenos*, and the one of our father, Saint Francis, they immediately arose, well and healed. More than two hundred of the latter were counted. In this manner the Indians were strongly confirmed in our holy Catholic faith.

The friars, although they did not see the nun there, learned accurately from all the Indians how she had appeared visibly to everyone and had instructed them in their own tongue and reproved them for being lazy because they did not come to seek us. At that very moment, there came ambassadors from other neighboring nations, such as the Quiviras and Xapies, also pleading for baptism, because the same nun had preached to them. These friars left that miraculous conversion in this state and returned to give us an account of what they had seen and to obtain more workers and helpers to build a church there. Thus we were all convinced that this nun was the mother María de

Jesús mentioned in the report of the archbishop, and that she was the one who had been privileged to be God's apostle in that miraculous way.

When I arrived in Spain in 1630, the most reverend general of the order, fray Bernardino de Zena, reassured me that it was she, that he had investigated this matter eight years previously when he was commissary general in Spain, and that the nun was miraculously carried to the conversion in New Mexico. Therefore he gave me a special permit to visit her personally at Agreda and ordered her to satisfy me in every way to the glory and honor of God. She convinced me absolutely by describing to me all the things in New Mexico as I have seen them myself, as well as by other details which I shall keep within my soul. Consequently, I have no doubts in this matter whatsoever.

Likewise, Father fray Juan of Santander, who was commissary general of the Indies in the year 1630 when I arrived in Spain and who is now bishop of Mallorca, having heard about these things and the miracle which the blessed father, fray Francisco de Porras, performed at Moqui by giving sight to the child, blind from birth, with the aid of a cross from Mother Luisa de Carrión, convinced that she was the person mentioned in the memoir of the archbishop of Mexico, wanted to go personally to investigate this important incident at the villa of Carrión. After he had communicated with Father fray Domingo de Aspe, confessor of the said mother, a friar of great merit and zeal—which are essential to govern so great a soul—the latter showed him the book of revelations which he is writing about her, a chapter describing how, a year and a half before I returned to Spain, Mother Luisa had been miraculously carried to the conversions in New Mexico. He took the actual passage from the book and showed it to me, but did not allow me to copy it.

Benavides to the Missionaries

Most dear and beloved father custodian and other friars of our father, Saint Francis, of the holy custodia of the Conversion of Saint Paul in the kingdoms and provinces of New Mexico:

I give infinite thanks to the divine majesty for having placed me, unworthy as I am, among the number enjoying the happy good fortune of your paternities, since you are so deserving of heavenly favor that the angels and our father, Saint Francis, aid you. They personally, truly, and actually carry the blessed and blissful Mother María de Jesús, discalced Franciscan of the order of Concepción, from the town of Agreda, which is in the limits of Castile, to help us with her presence and preaching in all these provinces and barbarous nations. Your paternities remember very well that in the year 1628, when I was prelate there and your servant, I exerted myself, although it must have been especially directed by heaven, to go to New Spain and report to the viceroy and the reverend prelates of the more notable and unusual things that were happening in their holy custodia.

Having carried out this task, upon my arrival in Mexico the viceroy and the reverend prelates agreed that I should go to Spain to inform his Majesty, as the source of everything, and our father general. Being so Catholic and zealous for the salvation of souls, they bestowed a thousand favors upon me for the good news I brought them, in regard to the spreading of our holy faith, the apostolic zeal with which your paternities labor in those conversions, and the temporal increment which the divine majesty has revealed as a reward for the zeal with which the king, our lord, favors and aids us.

With this letter I am forwarding to your paternities a printed Memorial which I presented to his Majesty and the royal Council of the Indies. It was so well received in Spain that I am planning to bring out a second printing for the satisfaction of the many who ask for it. Your paternities, please do not judge me inadequate, as I know very well that the Memorial is greatly so, considering how much it lacks and how much your paternities deserve. I prepared it in such brief form, even at the cost of not saying the many things that it does not contain, only to induce his Majesty to read it. They liked it so well that not only did they read it many times and learn it by heart, but they have repeatedly asked me for other copies. To satisfy these demands I have distributed four hundred copies. Our reverend father general sent some to Rome to his Holiness, in addition to the ones that I mentioned in the printed Memorial.

The times I have spoken to his Majesty and to his royal Council of the Indies, where ordinarily the affairs of the Indies are transacted, I have verbally and by many written testimonials in my hand told of what is transpiring in New Mexico. Here there was scanty information of New Mexico, as if God had not created it in this world. For this reason they did not know or appreciate how your paternities labor with apostolic zeal in that vineyard of the Lord. I hope in His divine majesty to be back among your paternities to enjoy the happy good fortune of your company, although I confess I do not deserve it, and to bring to your paternities and to all that land very great favors from his Holiness and the king, our lord, for the solace of all and the spreading of the divine name.

When I arrived in Spain, which was on August 1, 1630, as soon as our reverend father general, fray Bernardino de Sena [Siena], now bishop of Viseo, who is governing the order until the meeting of the general chapter—I repeat, as soon as he learned of my report of the blessed nun who goes about there preaching our holy Catholic faith in the manner your paternities know, his reverence told me at once that when he was commissary for Spain, before he became general, more than eight years ago, he received information that Mother María de Jesús, abbess of her convent in the town of Agreda, on the border between Aragon and Castile, had had some visions and accounts of the province in New Mexico. With the report I gave him and the one that had been sent to us at this time by the archbishop of Mexico, Don Francisco Manso, our reverend father general was inspired by such tenderness and devotion that he wanted to set out for the said town of Agreda, because the same thing I related had been told by Mother María de Jesús herself in the said years before, when he went in person to visit her convent, for it is under the jurisdiction of the order and the province of Burgos.

Face to face, Mother María de Jesús herself told the same story to our reverend father general, and now it was confirmed by what I told him. Since his many occupations did not permit him to go, he ordered me to look into it personally. He gave me authority to constrain the blessed nun through obedience to reveal to me all that she knew about New Mexico. I left this capital to fulfill this commission, arriving at Agreda on the last day of April, 1631.

First of all, I must state that María de Jesús, present abbess of the convent of Conception, can not be twenty-nine years of age yet. She has a beautiful face, very white, although rosy, with large black eyes. Her habit, and that of all the nuns in that convent—they number twenty-nine in all—is just the same as our habit. It is made of coarse gray sackcloth, worn next to the skin, without any other tunic, skirt, or underskirt. Over this gray habit comes the one of white sackcloth, coarse, with a scapulary of the same material, and the cord of our father, Saint Francis. Over the scapulary there is a rosary. They wear no sandals or any other footwear except some boards tied to their feet, or some hemp sandals. Their cloak is of heavy blue sackcloth. They wear a black veil.

I will not stop to tell of the strictness of this venerable mother and her convent, but only of that which concerns New Mexico. When I am worthy of seeing your paternities, of which I have great desire and hope, then I will tell about the marvelous things that our Lord brings about over there. Among other virtues that God granted this blessed mother is the eagerness for salvation of souls. From childhood she felt great grief for those who are damned, and particularly for the heathen, who, because of the lack of light and preachers, do not know God, our Lord. His Majesty revealed to her all the savage nations in the world that do not know Him, and she was transported by the aid of the angels that she has as guardians. Her wings are Saint Michael and our father, Saint Francis. She has preached in person our holy Catholic faith in every nation, particularly in our New Mexico, where she was carried in the same manner. The custodian angels of its provinces also came in person to get her by command of God, our Lord. The habit she wore most frequently was that of our father, Saint Francis; on other occasions it was that of La Concepción, together with the veil. However, she always wore the white sleeves rolled up, and the skirts of her white habit drawn up, so that the gray showed a great deal. The first time that she went was in the year 1620, and she has continued these visits so often that there were days when she appeared three and four times in less than twenty-four hours. This has continued without interruption until 1631.

My dear fathers, I do not know how to express to your paternities the impulses and great force of my spirit when this blessed Mother told me that she had been present with me at the baptism of the Pizos

[Piros] and that she recognized me as the one she had seen there. Likewise she had helped Father fray Cristóbal Quirós with some baptisms, giving a minute description of his person and face, even saying that although he was old he did not show any gray hair, but that he was long-faced and ruddy; that once when the father was in his church baptizing, many Indians came in and all crowded around the door and that she with her own hands pushed them on, getting them to their places so that they would not hinder him; that they looked to see who was pushing them and they laughed when they were unable to see who did it; that she pushed them on so that they would push the others, etc.

She also told me all we know that has happened to our brothers and fathers, fray Juan de Salas and fray Diego López, in the journeys to the Jumanas, and that she asked the latter and instructed them to go and call the fathers, as they did. She gave me all their descriptions, adding that she assisted them. She knows Captain Tuerto very well, giving a detailed description of him, and of the others. She herself sent the emissaries from Quivira to call the fathers. The Indians themselves will testify to all of this, as she speaks to them in person. She described to me also the trip of Father Ortega, who was so fortunate as to save his life through the signs he found, all of which she mentioned to me. When she turned from the north to the east, she set out from a region of intense cold until reaching a warm and pleasant climate, and in that direction onward, although very far off, are those magnificent kingdoms, but that our father, Saint Francis, is conquering it all. She told me so many details of this country that I did not even remember them myself, and she brought them back to my mind. I asked her why she did not allow us to see her when she granted this bliss to the Indians. She replied that they needed it and we did not, and that her blessed angels arranged everything. However, I trust in divine providence that by the time this letter reaches the hands of your paternities some of you will have succeeded in seeing her, for I asked it of her most earnestly, and she promised she would ask God, and that if He granted it, she would do it most willingly.

She said that by setting out from Quivira to the east, although very far away, one would pass the threatening death signs seen by Father Ortega along the way so that our holy faith should not get there, for so it had been arranged by the devil; that many could be converted along the way if the soldiers would set a good example *res valde difficilis, sed omnia deo facilia*; that our father, Saint Francis, obtained a pledge from God, our Lord, that the Indians would become converted merely at the sight of our friars. God be infinitely praised for so many blessings.

I should indeed like to tell your paternities in this letter everything that the venerable Mother told me, but it is not possible. Nevertheless I have written down a great deal of it in a book which I shall bring with me for the consolation of all. She said that after traveling those long and difficult roads from the east one would come to the kingdoms of Chillescas, Cambujos, and Jumanas, and then to the kingdom of Titlas; that these names are not the real ones, but something resembling them, because although when among them she speaks their language, away from there she does not know it nor is it revealed to her. That kingdom of Titlas, very large and very densely populated, is the one most frequently visited by her. Through her intercession our father, Saint Francis, led two friars of our order there. They baptized the king and many people, and there they were martyred. She says that they were not Spaniards; and that they martyred also many Christian Indians. The king preserves their bones in a silver box in the church that was built there. Once she took from here a chalice for consecration, and the friars used it for saying mass and for carrying the blessed sacrament in procession. All of this will be found there, as well as many crosses and rosaries that she distributed. She was martyred and received many wounds, and her heavenly angels crowned her, wherefore she attained martyrdom from our Lord.

Thus it seems to me this letter will suffice so that your paternities may be comforted in your labors by such a companion and saint. The Lord will grant that I come among your paternities so that you may learn of the things in the manner she has told them to me. I showed them to her in order that she should tell me if I had erred in anything and whether it was as had transpired between the two of us. To this effect I invoked the obedience from our most reverend father general that I carried for this purpose, and it was invoked also by the reverend father provincial of that province, her confessor, there present. Since it seems to me that her answer is going to bring your paternities great consolation and encouragement, as it has done around here, for the whole of Spain wants to move thither, I shall transcribe here what she replied in her handwriting. I retain the original to take it to your paternities and to all the provinces, naming each one of you by name. I have also the very habit that she wore when she went there. The veil radiates such a fragrance that it is a comfort to the spirit.

Sor María's Letter to the Missionaries

I obey what your reverence, our father general; our father, fray Sebastián Marcilla, provincial of this holy province of Burgos; our father, fray Francisco Andrés de la Torre, who is the one who governs my soul; and your paternity, my father custodian for New Mexico, have asked me to tell in the name of your paternity whether that which is contained in these notebooks is what I have said, discussed, consulted, and talked about to your paternity concerning what the mercy of God and His just and immutable decisions have worked in my simple heart. Perhaps He chooses the most insignificant and unworthy individual to show the strength of His mighty hand so that the living may know that all things derive from the hand of the Father of Light dwelling on high, and that we attain everything through the power and strength of the Almighty. And so I say that this is what befell me in the provinces of New Mexico, Quivira, the Jumanas, and other nations, although these were not the first kingdoms where I was taken by the will of God. By the hand and aid of His angels I was carried wherever they took me, and I saw and did all that I have told the father, and other things which, being numerous, it is not possible to narrate in order to enlighten all those nations in our holy Catholic faith. The first ones where I went are toward the east, I believe, and one must travel in that direction to reach them from the kingdom of Quivira. I call these kingdoms with reference to our way of speaking, Titlas, Chillescas, and Caburcos, which have not been discovered. To reach them it seems to me that one will meet with great obstacles on account of the many kingdoms which intervene, inhabited by very warlike people who will not allow the passing of the Christian Indians from New Mexico, whom they distrust, and especially do they distrust the friars of our holy father, Saint Francis, because the devil has deceived them, making them believe that there is poison where the antidote is, and that they will become vassals and slaves if they become Christians, when it constitutes their liberty and happiness in this world. It seems to me that the way to succeed would be to send friars of our father, Saint Francis, and for their security and protection to require that they be accompanied by soldiers of good repute and habits, men who forbear patiently the abuse that may come upon them. By example and patience, every-thing can be endured, as the example helps very much. By discover-ing these provinces great work will have been done in the vineyard of the Lord.

The events which I have reported happened to me from the year 1620 to the present year, 1631, in the kingdoms of Quivira and the Ju-manas, which were the last ones where I was transported and which, your paternity says, were discovered by the very persons of those holy padres through their good intelligence. I entreat, advise, and urge them in behalf of the Lord to labor in such a blessed task, praising the Most High for their good fortune and bliss, which are great indeed. For his Majesty appoints you His treasurers and disbursers of His pre-cious blood and places in your hands its price, which is the souls of so many Indians, who, lacking light and someone to furnish it to them continue in darkness and blindness and are deprived of the most holy and desirable of the immaculate, tender, and delightful law and of the blessing of eternal salvation. The said padres must outdo them-selves in this field of the Lord to please the Most High, for the harvest is abundant and the workers are few and they must exercise the great-est possible charity with these creatures of the Lord, made in His im-age and likeness with a rational soul to enable them to know Him.

Do not allow, my dear fathers and lords, that the wishes of the Lord and His holy will be frustrated and permitted to fail because of the many sufferings and hardships, for the Almighty will reply that He has His delights and joys with the sons of men. Since God created these Indians as apt and competent beings to serve and worship Him, it is not just that they lack what we, the rest of the Christian faithful, possess and enjoy. Rejoice then, my dear fathers, for the Lord has given you the opportunity, occasion, and good fortune of the apostles. Do not let it go to waste because of considerations of difficulty. Remember your duty to obey the Almighty and to extend and plant His holy law regardless of the hardships and persecutions you may suffer in the emulation of your Master.

I can assure your paternities that I know with all exactness and light that the blessed ones envy you, if envy could exist among them, which is impossible, but I am stating it thus, according to our mode of expression. If they could forsake their eternal bliss to accompany you in those conversions, they would do it. This does not surprise me, for, as they see in the Lord, who is the main cause and object of their bliss and the voluntary mirror in which all recognize themselves, the special bliss enjoyed by the apostles and for which they stand out over the other saints on account of what they have suffered for the conversion of souls; for this reason they would leave the enjoyment of God for the conversion of one soul. This will be a reason for your paternities availing yourselves of the opportunity that offers itself to you. I confess that if I could buy it with my blood, life, or cruel sufferings, I would do it, for I envy the good fortune of your paternities. Because, although the Most High grants that I may attain this fruit in my life, it is not on a course where I may suffer as much as your paternities, nor that I deserve anything, since my imperfections prevent it. But since I am helpless, I offer with all my heart and soul to help those of this holy community with prayers and pious exercises. I beg my affectionate padres to accept my good will and desire and to let me partake of some of the minor tasks and undertakings carried on by your paternities in those conversions. I shall appreciate it more than whatever I do by myself, as the Lord will be highly pleased by the conversion of souls. This very thing I have seen in the Almighty, and I have heard His blessed angels tell me that they envied the custodians of souls who devote themselves to conversions. As ministers who present our deeds to the Most High, they affirm that the ones His Majesty accepts with greatest satisfaction are those who are occupied in the conversions of New Mexico. The reason for this, the blessed angel explained, is that as the blood of the Lamb was sufficient for all souls and that He suffered for one what He suffered for all, the Lord grieved more over the loss of one soul through lack of knowledge of our holy faith than over enduring as many martyrdoms and deaths as He created souls. This should encourage such a holy occupation as well as much suffering to succeed in it.

As all that has been stated in my writing and that of my father custodian of New Mexico is true, being constrained by obedience, I signed it with my name. And I beg your paternities, all those I have mentioned here, in the name of the Lord himself, whom we serve and through whom I reveal this to you, to conceal and keep these secrets to yourselves, as the case demands that it should not be revealed to any living being.

From this house of the Concepción Purísima of Agreda, May 15, 1631, Sor María de Jesús.

Benavides' Letter on His Interview with Sor María

My dear fathers and brothers: I should very much have liked to write here for your greater consolation the many things I have recorded both by my hand and by that of this saintly mother regarding what our Lord has done through her in our behalf and support in those conversions. However, they are more to be retained in the heart than to be recorded. It seems to me that your paternities will feel relieved with the preceding accounts, which are all in her hand and signature, which I retain in my possession, as her style and thought, it is clearly seen, are evangelical.

I asked her whether we were proceeding in the right way in our conversions, not only in the buildings but also in the fields planted and whatever else is being done for the support and protection of the Indians. She replied that everything was very pleasing to our Lord, as it was all directed to the aim of the conversions, which is the greatest charity. She has earnestly taken it upon herself to commend your paternities to God, and also the peace and harmony between the governors and the friars, and to intercede for the conversions. Thus she commends everyone to God very earnestly, so that friars, governors, Spaniards, and Indians together and in harmony may worship and praise the Lord and above all may dedicate themselves to the bringing of the light of our holy Catholic faith to all those barbarous nations. Since His divine majesty employs us in that holy task let us not falter and fail by not withstanding everything and every occasion when we meet with opposition.

I realize also, dear fathers, that never did I deserve, because of my imperfections and limitations, to enjoy such peace as I desired. Nevertheless, I hope through the divine majesty that I may end whatever days He may grant me in the company and services of your paternities. His divine majesty knows how earnestly I desire it.

Your paternities please commend me greatly to all those Spanish gentlemen. Knowing that they have always had a kindly disposition toward me, I repay it fully by telling, as I have done, his royal Majesty and his royal Council of the Indies that they are true apostolic soldiers, both in the courage and good example with which they accompany us, whereby his Majesty considers himself well served. He promised to grant me whatever favor I asked in their behalf. The most important thing is that they must consider themselves fortunate in being protected by the blessed spirit of María de Jesús. She has seen them and commends them to God. So I thank them a thousand times, and God, for their being deserving. I have likewise told the Mother of the Christian spirit and virtue of all those Spanish women, of the humility and care with which they look after the neatness of the altars, and she said she also commends them to our Lord. I am also asking for the prayers of everyone.

I am sending likewise my congratulations for all the Indians, for they command her principal affection, because she goes to those remote and distant kingdoms; and, like spiritual children, to whom she has preached our holy Catholic faith and illuminated the darkness of their idolatry, she keeps them ever in mind in order never to forget them in her prayers. Blessed be such a land, and blessed be its fortunate inhabitants, since they command so many favors from heaven.

Your paternities' humble servant and son, fray Alonso de Benavides.

Our most reverend father general sends from here to your paternities his blessing together with that of our father, Saint Francis, for, as such true sons of his, you devote yourselves to such an apostolic task. He has instructed me to express this wish to your paternities.

Text of the Report to Father Manero

227   O   ur Most Reverend Father fray Pedro Manero, General Director of the Order of Our Father Saint Francis:

228   I confess at the feet of Your Reverence that my fault is worthy of reprimand, for I did not comply as fully as I ought when Your Reverence, on entering office, and our director of the Indies, when I still had him, instructed me to make a statement on the matter of my beginnings and the events in New Mexico. It was not my intention to disobey Your Reverence, but rather a desire that no memory of me remain in this vale of tears and that time might erase the one about which the order has not been careful, much to my dismay. But seeing myself bound by obedience, I shall briefly, clearly, and distinctly say what that was, as best I may be able to remember after so many years.

229   Ever since the Lord, moved only by his goodness and compassion, called me to fix my attention on his light and greater perfection in his service, there has been growing in me a keen desire to put them into action. This happened in the house of my parents at a very young age, and to the good upbringing and teaching they gave me I attribute, second only to God's grace, all good things of mine, for from the age of nine or ten they made their children pray in constant devotions and had us engage in mental prayer, for which they withdrew into their bedrooms and indicated another for me to do the same. Ever since the age I have mentioned, it seems the Lord filled my inner life with light, and it was like placing a little girl at the start of an exceedingly straight road and path and saying to me, "Here you are to walk without deviating or turning aside."

Then a brilliant light was revealed to me so I might see what I was to do on that road. I often explain this light by comparing it to the nature of the physical light that shines on us all. So like the day, which from the first twilight of the dawn grows until noon, from my child-

hood to the state in which I am now, this inner brightness has increased. This has been the lamp of the lamb guiding me day and night
in prosperity and adversity, in struggle and in peace. This day dawned
for me and its light began to guide me since I was a little girl, while
later it illuminated my way as a nun and still goes on growing. I did
not feel that it grew dark or went out in the three years during which
I received outwardly visible signs of God's grace, which began the
year of my novitiate.

230   Through his kindness alone, the Lord gave me a receptive nature
in spiritual matters that allowed me easily to turn my mind to meditation on the Lord and the mysteries of our holy faith that my parents
were teaching me. And ever since I was a little girl, but even more
after becoming a nun, I found that when I focused my attention within,
I would enter a state of exceedingly quiet prayer. I longed to be a nun
and wife of Our Savior Christ and asked Him earnestly to arrange for
that to happen. His Majesty did it in such a wonderful way that He
placed my parents and brothers and sisters in the perfection of monastic life, making my parents' house the church where we put on the
habit. Feeling so grateful and obliged for all these kindnesses from the
Lord, and as I am naturally affectionate and intense, I let myself be
carried away by the first waves of feeling, for the strength of reason
could not hold them back, and my constitution was not robust enough
to resist them; my judgment, too, was not capable of or accustomed
to choosing between letting my dazzled feelings go or reining them in.
Out of the tension between my fear and desire came some trances, it
seeming to me that my chest was bursting with the effects of love's
deep affection; I would struggle to resist but always ended giving in to
the power of the love.

231   Then as the Most High, moved only by his goodness, cast light
into my understanding so that I might know the articles of the faith
and good and evil, He instilled in me such an intense unhappiness at
the thought there are souls that are damned that I would faint away,
and my pain grew greater when I learned there were souls who do not
confess our holy faith. These feelings greatly increased when I became
a nun, although ever since I was a little girl I often experienced them.
After putting on the habit, my burning desire for God's love grew
stronger. I would become sentimental, cry, and sob. My heart seemed

to be bursting out of my chest, and pining and exhausted, I would go
to the most out-of-the-way areas of the house to hide and pour out
my feelings where no one could see me. I would lose contact with the
world around me, and as at that time I was ignorant of the dangers
these outward signs bring, I gave free rein to the feelings and let myself be carried away, or more precisely, I was unable to resist the Lord,
and so the others discovered that I stopped talking and went into
trances. Father fray Juan de Torrecilla, my first confessor, someone
more well intentioned than careful, began to question me and talk
publicly about all this.

My misfortunes reached the point that once after I took communion, they raised my veil and some lay people saw my face, and since
everything related to raptures makes such a splash in the heedless
world, the publicity surrounding this expanded and went forward.
The nuns who were my superiors were extremely fond of this business
of outward signs of holiness; they made commitments to various lay
people, and once they had allowed some to see, they did not want to
say no to others. I was told of this by someone sick who had come to
the convent, supposedly crazy, though in my opinion thoroughly sane.
So sharp were my bitterness and pain at this discovery that I made a
vow not to receive Our Lord without shutting myself into the lower
choir, which was the place where we took communion. I obtained a
padlock from outside the house, put it in place, and locked myself
in; I was able to do this because I took communion alone due to the
many illnesses I had. Other times, they would take the key away from
me; then I would drink or take syrup so they would not compel me to
receive Our Lord, it seeming better to go without that comfort than to
do something so unwise as to show myself to everyone who came to
see, for just hearing the noise of them all made me faint. They repri-
manded me harshly and told me I was disobedient, so I would relent
in order to obey.

232   They freed me of the vow to shut myself in, or they commuted
it, but then since I had heard it said that vows made in the hands of
an abbess could not be lifted, one day I spoke to her privately and
managed to make her agree that in her hands I would take a vow not
to take the most holy sacrament without shutting myself in so that
the nuns would not enter to take off my veil or bring me closer to the

place where we receive communion for people to see me; I used to move back from it even though I was unable to go up to my cell. Later I found out that after I was now able to shut myself in again, they took a piece out of the door of the lower choir stalls in order to go in and place me on display, afterwards fitting the boards back into place so that I would not notice.

This is common knowledge among the senior nuns that go back to that time, during which God filled me with such intense hatred of these outward signs that they put me through the pains of martyrdom. And God filled me with such regret about them that if officers of the civil law had caught me committing serious crimes and taken me through the streets on a donkey to be exposed to public shame, I would not have felt as much humiliation as I did at people seeing me in those moments of seclusion and spiritual elevation. I would weep and cry out to God, asking Him to give me great faith, hope, love of Him, and true humility, and to take away those outward signs.

233   Under these trials, my love grew even stronger, and in them the generosity of the Most High more generous. He let me see the mysteries of our holy faith and what He had suffered for our souls and that many are lost, and the pain of it all was breaking my heart. The fact that God's creatures should be damned, including my neighbors, who for me are brothers and sisters, has shattered my soul with sorrow. What I have gone through is more than could be told or even exaggerated; such concern and loving wishes for the good of other souls and their salvation could not possibly seem to be anything except a gift of God, for vile dust like me, who could never by herself do anything good, would not have been able to engender this love for one's neighbor.

At this time and in this state of mind, it happened that the Lord would let me know occasionally that He wanted me to work on behalf of his creatures and for the welfare of their souls. I would call on his compassion and offer to suffer more and give my life if that were necessary so that just one soul might be saved.

234   It seems to be that it was the day after having received Our Lord that His Majesty showed me the whole world, or so it appeared to me, by means of abstract images, and I perceived the variety of created things and how astonishing the Lord is in the universal diversity of

the earth. With great clarity, He would show me the throng of creatures with souls that exist, and how few of them confess the pure
faith and go through baptism's door to become children of the Holy
Church. My heart would split when I saw that the abundant redemp-
tion did not fall on more than just a very few. I perceived the fulfillment of the Gospel, that many are called and few are chosen. The
Almighty created them all so they might know and love Him, but
there are only a few who confess the faith, as one can see by the many
pagans, idolaters, Moors, and heretics there are.

Seeing all this caused me bitter and unbearable pain, with which
my requests and anxious concern for other souls went on growing.
Among the many different peoples who neither recognized nor confessed the faith, as the Lord let me see, He told me that the creatures
most disposed to convert, the ones toward whom his compassion was
then most inclined, were the New Mexicans and the inhabitants of
other remote kingdoms in that part of the world. No sooner had the
Most High revealed to me his will in this matter than my intense feelings of love for God and my neighbor were renewed, and I called out
from the innermost part of my being on behalf of those souls.

235   Another day after having received Our Lord, it seemed to me
that His Majesty was showing me in greater detail those kingdoms
and Indians that His Majesty wished converted, and He commanded
me to ask and work on their behalf. And the information I was getting was clearer and more detailed as regards the sort of people and
their appearance, their inclinations, and the need for ministers to set
them on the path to knowledge of God and his holy faith. All of this
confirmed and strengthened my desire and longing to work and ask.
Another time, too, those kingdoms were shown to me in detail, with
the features and properties of that part of the world, the appearance
of the men and women, their differences in many things from people
here, and other circumstances; it seemed to me I addressed them and
begged them to go seek ministers of the Gospel to teach them the catechism and baptize them, and I came to know them, too. The way this
happened is something I do not feel I can explain nor do I remember
clearly.

236   A report or paper was done eight years, more or less, after this
happened, on the occasion of Father Alonso de Benavides, director of

New Mexico, having returned to Spain, and he did it with other grave fathers who were from this province. About some things it is accurate, while about others they have added and exaggerated; it is not believable that the fault lies with such good fathers who take their responsibilities so seriously, but it results rather from the fact they gathered their information from nuns and friars, for I was always most guarded about making statements on these matters except in the secrecy of the confessional. And since it was a question of making a statement that would go to a great many people, and I wanted to be cautious, it saddened me that they gave greater credence to people I had dealt with; as the story was transmitted through so many friars and nuns, it was unavoidable that the truth of it would be adulterated, especially on a subject where imprudent religious enthusiasts feel one is doing something grand by adding on more, but what gets added on is usually illegitimate, dangerous, harmful, and offensive to the truly pious. I have been unlucky because they have raised up many testimonies about me, saying more than has really occurred and happened to me; throughout my life this has caused anguish and suffering.

237   While in the state I have described, the things found in that notebook of Father Benavides did happen to me, and they reproduce the testimony given by Father fray Francisco Andrés and the other fathers, but one must remember that some of the things have been exaggerated or misunderstood, and others added. What the truth is I shall here state as best I may be able, although after so much time has gone by, I have lost the mental images of the event and very much forgotten it; the fact that I was so young when it happened to me fills me with even more doubt and perplexity. Drawing on the better understanding of things I have now that I am older, it seems to me that either it was all the work of my imagination or that God showed me those things by means of abstract images of the kingdoms and what was going on there, or perhaps that they were shown to me there. Neither then nor now was, or am, I capable of knowing the way it happened, but since it was generally known that the Indians were converting, in order to console and encourage me in my bitter distress that there should be souls lost who do not confess the faith, the Lord (to put it in terms we can understand) gave me reason to believe, in

the way He thought best, that some souls were, in fact, converting and would convert.

To both the Lord and my confessors I revealed a keen desire to die, if it were possible, so that I might address and convert those souls. After so much time has gone by, I cannot say how far it went or what I said or what they thought of me until Father fray Alonso de Benavides, director in Mexico, came to see me, for it happened twenty-nine years ago, more or less, when I was about twenty and inexperienced. It is possible that, in my ignorance, what was shown to me in the ways I have mentioned I might have mistaken for actually being there, that I may have recounted and described my desire to address them as preaching in fact.

238   Whether or not I really and truly went in my body is something about which I cannot be certain. And it is not surprising I have questions in my mind, for Saint Paul understood things better than I and yet tells us that he was carried up to the third heaven but does not know whether it was in his body or out of it. What I can assure you beyond any doubt is that the case did in fact happen, and that as far as I know, it had nothing to do with the devil or wrong desires. This I will affirm once, twice, or many times. I will not stop here to tell the story again, for it is all in that report. I shall just give the reasons tending to support the opinion that the trips happened to me in my body, as well as those that point to an angel, and then I shall state the things in that report that were invented.

239   In support of the opinion that I was really making the trips is the circumstance, which the fathers must have found convincing, that I saw each one of the kingdoms clearly and knew their names, they appearing to my understanding individually (these are the ones that appear in the report), and that I saw the cities and recognized the differences between them and the ones here, and that the climate and weather were different—warmer.

240   Their foods were primitive, and for light they used wooden torches. I would address them and explain all the articles of faith, exhorting them and teaching the catechism. They were receptive to all of this and sort of bowed, acclaiming the great good they were receiving and making entreaties.

241   And although this is true, I have always questioned the idea that it happened to me in my body, the case being so extraordinary and unusual. For that reason, in the statements I have made, I express doubts and distrust. I did not bring anything back from there, and even supposing it really happened and I could have, I would have refrained, for the Lord cast light into my mind and taught me that not by thought, word, or deed should I go so far as to long for or touch anything except as the will of God would be pleased. In all outward and bodily things, there is greater danger, for as the devil is not master of the inner self, he aims for victory through the senses. Outwardly, too, I was unable to perceive how I moved or whether I was carried; as I was in trances or raptures, it was quite impossible.

242   Still, it seems to me that at times I would see the world at night in some places while in others it was day, in some the weather was calm and in others rainy, and I beheld the sea and its beauty. But all of this could very well have been the effect of the Lord showing it to me, for as his light and intelligence are so fertile, quick, and bright, He might have merely shown it to me, and still I perceived it with perfect clarity.

243   It seems to me that on one occasion I gave the Indians some rosaries. I had them with me and distributed them among them, then I never saw the rosaries again. This is something I do not think I have ever talked about until right now, unless it was to Father Benavides. The way in which I am most inclined to believe this happened and that seems most credible to me was, or is, that an angel, taking on my looks, appeared there and preached and taught them the catechism, while here the Lord showed me what was going on there as an answer to my prayers. For the Indians seeing me there was true, according to Father Benavides, and that is the reason I feel it was an angel with my looks. I also learned about the wars they made, and that they did not fight with weapons like the ones used here, but with machines for throwing stones, similar to slings, and with crossbows and wooden knives. And it seems to me that while the war was going on, I was praying with my hands raised on their behalf and feeling pity for their trials.

244   On other occasions, it seemed to me that I was telling them to convert, that just as they differed in nature from the animals, they

should differ from them by knowing their Creator and by coming into the Holy Church through the door of baptism, whereupon they would become imbued with the habits of faith, hope, and charity and come to know their God.

245   Still, when all is said and done, I have to ask myself why the Most High would have chosen an instrument as base and low as myself. When I take a look at myself, I feel it must have been only in my mind, that, yes, all this is imaginary; I fear the worst.

246   I can be sure only that it does not come from the devil, for I know my will has been free of such things and that my intentions have been good, and their effects as well.

247   What I take issue with in that notebook is their telling me that they wrote it down on my orders, when the truth is that I went along with it passively, not actively, and that I was horribly pained that the report was put together. I was trembling, beside myself with anxiety, and never realized what I was signing; I did not even pay attention to it. The truth is I left everything in the hands of those highly responsible fathers, entrusting the success of my affairs to them more than to myself, for they were prelates and scholars. For all these reasons I did not pay attention to what I signed.

248   There is also an *exordium* or exhortation in my name. It is true that I wrote it to encourage the friars in the New World and privately gave it to the director, Father Benavides. I thought not a creature would see it. He says that Saint Michael and Our Father Saint Francis would accompany me, and that I said they were my wings and that Saint Michael used to go on the right side.

249   That was a remark of mine in conversation. I said they were my wings, calling them that metaphorically and reflecting that just as wings help birds to fly, just so the intercession of Our Father Saint Francis and of Saint Michael help us fly to God. Among nuns, it is common to call the holy angel and Our Father Saint Francis wings, for we have them placed on either side of the church, and they are our patrons and advocates. But Father Benavides understood it so literally that he thought they were wings that would always accompany me, turning my devout feelings into a mystery. And although I have received many favors from the glorious prince Saint Michael and Our Father Saint Francis and owe them much, and in many difficult mo-

ments have seen him and the holy angel, they have not accompanied me as Father Benavides claims.

250   He also states I had seen two friars wearing extraordinary habits, that they were of our order, and that going there had been a miracle; it is true I saw them in the way he says, marveling that they had traveled so far. But I do not think I said they had been miraculously transported, for as the Indians came to ask for baptism, and ministers to teach and baptize them, those friars could have reached there after much time and effort. From this I can see he took the words I used in their natural sense and made them into a mystery of divine revelation.

251   He speaks, too, of Mother María de Cristo in Madrid. She is a nun in the Caballero de Gracia convent that is attached to the court, and after this case, which went on during the administration of the founders of this convent, who were from Burgos and subsequently left, she came to reform this house, staying four years. She told him I had taken to the kingdoms of the New World a monstrance containing unconsecrated communion wafers to supply the lack of things needed for saying Mass there. I shall explain what really happened in this incident of the monstrance.

252   They often lacked the things necessary for saying Mass, it is true, and became despondent at not having them as well; I was aware of this, and that the friars were despondent and depressed, complaining for that reason. I told it to my confessors, and they must have told it to the abbess and the teacher, who were from Burgos and died many years ago. They were very kind but extremely fond of these sensational topics, and they often instructed me to take things to the kingdoms, and other times they suggested I do some wonders; if the Lord had not warned me not to do or attempt anything, I might have done many foolish things.

So one day they ordered me to take a monstrance containing communion wafers that the missionaries might say Mass and make a procession. But for my part, I was afraid to do something like that and touch the monstrance in which our Lord had been; I returned it to its place. But I did not dare to be openly disobedient for they were disgusted with me because of other things I was not doing and because of shutting myself into the lower choir; then in the confusion, the nuns lost track of the monstrance and must have thought I took it with me. When Mother María de Cristo came to refound the community, the nuns must have told her about it, she having recently arrived, along with other sensational items. Since she went back to Madrid after four years, she must later have told Father Benavides about it, as he says. But the fact is that I did not take the monstrance, told my confessors that, and they approved of my decision. They do make processions with the most holy sacrament and with great devotion, and I did see them some times, but I find the events in Father Benavides' report all mixed up.

253   He says, too, that I have more than one guardian angel. I cannot deny I owe a lot to angelical nature and have received many kindnesses through their ministry to me, and that some, appointed by the Lord, accompanied me during the time when I wrote the life of Our Lady, which I later burned. Without thinking it through carefully, I have referred to them as my guardians and protectors, recalling that psalm of David that I will quote: *"Angelis suis Deus mandavit de te, etc."*[17]

254   It seems to speak in the plural, "He sent his angels,"[18] and in the singular, "of you." From comments like these has come the statement that I have more than one guardian angel. But strictly speaking, one cannot talk about a guardian angel unless the angel has been present continuously, since birth, and for that reason I have stated that I do not have more than one guardian angel, for I would not be so vain as to claim that more was done for me than for others, especially since I deserve less.

255   During those three years, I do believe I wrote down the names of some angels and that I would have called them guardians and referred to them in the *Life of the Virgin*, for they were present with me while I was writing it. But it must be understood that they are not guardian angels, but given me only for that project or for other circumstances and trials.

256   Father Benavides' statement says further that it would have been five hundred times or more that I went to those kingdoms. I have already said that I do not know whether I really went or some angel for me. But if the number five hundred is taken to represent all the times I became aware of those kingdoms, in one way or another, or all the

times I prayed for or wanted their conversion, in that sense it is true, and the number would be even more than five hundred.

257   He says, moreover, that once I was there three days and that this happened other times. That is not true because I was never there (if I did go) a day and a night, nor was it necessary, because to teach them the catechism and instruct them in the faith and urge them to go look for missionaries, a few hours or one day was enough. The origin of it being said that I had been there for three days was that at that time I went through such bad periods of illness that I used to go three days without speaking or eating, or sometimes one, and they interpreted any of those incidents as my being off in the kingdoms. And when those fathers put together the report that Benavides wrote, the friars or nuns must have told them about this.

258   He says, moreover, that I gave him a veil calling it my husband's garment, and that it smelled good, and that I said the odor came from the contact my guardian angels had with me. Never in my life do I remember having said that it smelled good, and if I said such a thing, I would consider myself more puffed up with pride than Lucifer; I do not even remember giving him the veil. My natural mother was the doorkeeper and must have given it to him in my name, for she was more enthusiastic and fond of making people happy than she was cautious in these matters. It was not the veil I was using because I did not miss it; it must have been one of mine from the wardrobe. When it comes to people giving away personal things of mine, I have always been very scrupulous, for I know who I am.

For this reason, the whole time I have been abbess (which is twenty-three years now), I have obliged the nuns by their vows of holy obedience not to give away my personal things. As far as the odor goes, the nuns used to say, "Oh, what a good smell, Mother! There are angels here; Your Reverence is with the angels." This sort of conversation must have come to Benavides' ears, and that would be why he said it. As to the angels having contact, I do not know why an educated person would say angels had contact, when they are spiritual, perfect beings that by their very nature cannot have the earthiness we do, for we are made up of spirit and body while they are spirit only.

What I can assure you of in all truth is that no holy angel has ever touched my person or any part of it, nor have I ever seen them do anything but stand at a distance, serious, severe, and pure. My considered opinion of this whole case is that it actually happened, but the way and the "how" are not easily known since it happened so many years ago; since the Indians said they had seen me, either I myself or some angel who looked like me did go there.

259   That the truth was adulterated, the facts embroidered or changed, is nothing to marvel at, for the grave fathers who gathered the information and prepared the statement had not been my confessors when the case happened, and Father fray Francisco Andrés had only recently come. Being timid, I said little. They got their information from people who knew nothing more than a few words they had heard here and there, so it was impossible to purify the truth; they could only adulterate it. I signed without thinking about or paying attention to what I was doing. I have already said what was invented. All those names, the things that happened to Indians and friars, and all the rest in the notebook is not true. About how this happened, I have already said what I think.

5

The Crucible of Trials

A Vision of Confrontation

S or María died before she was able to put in order the complete body of her mystical expression. Still, in the prologue to at least three manuscripts of *Face of the Earth*, she includes a paragraph that can be taken as a projected table of contents, making clear that the cosmographical treatise had been integrated, at least in the planning stage, into a longer work that includes much more:

> The method and style I have used in writing this little work and its contents is to recount all the knowledge the Lord has shown me following the same order in which His Highness did it. It will be divided into three parts, as follows. The first will be to recount the knowledge that I have had of all things created, going from the empyrean heaven to the center of the earth and what principally is contained in it; to recount all there is from east to west and other mysteries that are too many for us creatures to know them all, all that the Lord created for mankind, to be used for our outer selves and as recreation for our senses. The second contains a recounting of the treasures and spiritual gifts that God transmits to us who are living in this valley of tears, and all that is contained in the church militant and what is the church and its treasures. The third contains all that belongs to the church triumphant, the hierarchy of the angels and the saints, as the Lord has assigned it to them. And after all these kinds of knowledge, the last one is knowledge of God, which I shall describe on the basis of a great and unmistakable kindness the Most High did for me in showing me His Highness in a special way.[1]

A second prologue, also written retrospectively, adds to our knowledge of the sorrows and consolations of Sor María's youth and how they flow into *The Mystical City of God*. She recalls her nostalgia for God's presence during the periods when He was silent for her, an emotional distress that aggravated the physical weaknesses and tensions of a difficult adolescence full of "sicknesses, sadness, and despair." But from Sor María's mature perspective, these sufferings were seen as only the necessary preparatory stage that cleans the spirit for the delight of heavenly communication. They make up what Sor María calls "the crucible of trials," the path of purification that in the classic mystic schema precedes illumination and, later, union. Kempe similarly believed that God showed her special grace because she had patiently endured tribulations, whereas priests and monks did not receive such grace because they were, she felt, unwilling to undergo so much suffering.[2]

Sor María offers encouragement, however, in her assertion that all who long to approach God along this path have reason to take heart in the knowledge that not only will the trials come to an end but also that providence gauges and moderates them to test and develop—without breaking—the strength available in each moment of spiritual development. While in our century the comparison may come to mind of a divine athletic trainer, the metaphor used by Sor María is very different but typical of her own society: "He has given me as much snow as my wool could take."

One should not think, Sor María is careful to add, that physical and emotional pain oblige God to grant the desired favors. It is not a question of cause and effect, as fasting and sleep deprivation can generate hallucinations, but rather of spiritual readiness, of receptivity, of the "qualities necessary for the Most High to act." The rejection of earthly desires—the focus of the quietism that Miguel de Molinos would popularize later in the century—fashions the cup but does not fill it. In Sor María's words, trials gratefully accepted "do not give blessings, but they predispose."

When after a period of eighty days God breaks his silence to her, she experiences a kind of bilocation, though not this time to the Southwest. An angel stays in her place while she leaves to undertake heroic exploits, this time going all the way to hell to confront a high-ranking demon, clearly representative of Satan, the anti-Christ. The legendary Cid, in confronting and bare-handedly caging the lion that got loose in his castle, could not have shown more courage.

As mentioned earlier, the Virgin herself, in several of the *cantigas* in her honor, similarly stayed in a nun's place in the convent while the nun went out, but the change from the New World to the Other World is significant. On her mission to the Southwest, Sor María was acting out a human role corresponding to her moment in history and the goals of her religious order. Now she takes on a larger dimension, overtly mythological and biblical. Throughout this memory from adolescence recaptured decades later, there is a well-defined foreshadowing of the grandiose deeds to come later in *The Mystical City of God*.

The stations of Sor María's personal cross and salvation are set on the same stage as the events of the Holy Scriptures, indicating that the visionary young woman was convinced she had something important to do in the drama of the human race. Among echoes of the Satanic dragon and the New Jerusalem of the Apocalypse, Sor María tells the story of Lucifer's fall and the fall of Adam and Eve to which it leads, culminating in tireless diabolical temptation of their descendants. But all is not lost, for sometimes men and women, strengthened by grace, manage to resist in spite of the most horrible traps hell can invent.

Such is the case of the heroic young nun, she tells us. Thanks only to supernatural help, which God Himself classifies as one of his greatest acts of kindness, Sor María overcomes the perverse strategies devised in infernal war councils convoked especially to destroy her. The action is remarkably like that in *Paradise Lost*, which gave English the word "pan-demonium," and the two narratives were written in the same years. Arenal and Schlau have documented that pervasive devils were believed to be the source of troubles of all kinds.[3]

Sor María's journey to the realm of darkness is not, therefore, without heroic significance. Like her bilocation to the American Southwest, it reflects Christ's descent into the underworld to combat evil and death. As in *The Mystical City of God*, there is a parallel between Jesus and the Virgin, and between the Virgin and Sor María, identifications that make Sor María something of a savior—of herself and of the readers to whom she communicates the life of the Virgin. In "The Crucible of Trials," which dramatizes and gives so much importance to the nun's temptations, a parallel, only half hidden, is suggested between her one-on-one with the demon and Christ's temptation in the desert. And when an angel announces on the day of the octave of the Assumption of the Virgin that God has arranged for one final, heroic test before Sor María will hear his voice directly, she answers following the model of a heavenly role model who in Sor María's biography becomes immensely less passive than in the gospel accounts of her: "Let his will be done in me, his handmaiden and slave." Readers of Kempe may be reminded of the parallel that the English mystic developed between herself and Mary Magdalene.[4]

The Agredan Style

The thematic importance of the "The Crucible of Trials" for the imaginative trajectory leading from *Face of the Earth* to the bilocation, and then to *The Mystical City of God*, has led me to translate and include it in this chapter. However, it is also useful as a short sample of Sor María's mature narrative style, which over the book's life has been commented on as an important part of its attraction. Although many readers in this century of Hemingway and haiku have found it wordy and overly rhetorical, that reaction was not typical in the past, when it was more likely to be called elegant, hieratic, and well suited to the book's sublime subjects. Pardo Bazán's condensation, in a more direct style, was no more successful at the turn of the century than the original she hoped to make more accessible to modern taste. Something important was lost in the paring down and rephrasing, just as the content of poetry is not separable from its form.

Face of the Earth, like *The Mystical City of God*, shows Sor María's ability to combine catalog-like order with emotional intensity. Her letter to Manero reveals her acuity in marshalling arguments. "The Crucible of Trials" illustrates the extent to which her style is graphic and representational. From the theological ideas of the times, Sor María, like Dante, creates an almost tangible world of images. Pérez Villanueva, who has explored connections between her writings and Spanish painting of the period, reminds us that many artists chose to represent the same visionary themes typical of Sor María's works, and that the styles are similar:

There is a correlation between the usual literary style [of the period], so descriptive and almost pictorial, and the pictures and graphic representations very much in vogue at that time. When Sor María de Agreda writes, "The Queen of Angels appeared to me, very lovely and beautiful, charmingly adorned," we are looking at the "Coronation of the Virgin" by Velázquez, in the Prado, or the "Immaculate Conception," in London, as he was representing it during those years, or as it was done in sculpture by his countryman Martínez Montañés. Velázquez himself offers us in his "St. John the Evangelist on Patmos," in the British National Gallery, a scene illustrative of the visionary mystics and monks of the period who experienced writing by divine inspiration while suspended between earthly reality and mystical rapture. A shared world of images transferred from dreamlike imagination to either the brush or the pen.[5]

Augustine M. Esposito, in a brief study of *The Mystical City of God*, argues that Sor María's biography of the Virgin—as well as being orthodox and repeatedly receiving the church's approbation—is good reading. Esposito addresses Sor María's style from the perspective of Mikhail Bahktin's "dialogical principle," and he points out that the Virgin takes on a greater appearance of reality and her personality becomes more vivid and engaging by virtue of conversing with Sor María.[6] A similar observation has been made about Jesus and Mary in Kempe's book, where they give the impression of being the author's close friends engaged in a private chat with her.[7] In this regard, a parallel might be drawn to part 2 of *Don Quixote*, in which part 1, whose physical reality the readers have held in their hands, is prominent as something the fictional characters have read. In both Cervantes' work and Sor María's, there is a mixing of fact and fiction—of book and author on the one hand and the personages of the imagination on the other—that creates a convincing literary world.

The Bible, the source of many of the themes of this prologue, is also an important stylistic influence. For example, Sor María often calls herself a lowly worm, a cliché of humility common in the period but having echoes in the psalms and the prophets. Such expressions are combined with a fear of enemies and a consciousness of not being able to defend oneself without the help of the Almighty. Weber has shown that in the writings of Teresa de Avila, such topoi of self-deprecation are in fact strategies of empowerment that gain acceptance for the truth, to be understood as divine, that the human writer, especially one who is hierarchically disadvantaged, cannot dare present on her own authority.[8] Kempe, too, uses language that emphasizes her smallness and imperfection, such as "sinful caitiff" and "vile wretch." Both she and Sor María stress their lowliness in relation to the Creator by referring to themselves as "this creature,"[9] yet both claim that extraordinary powers have been granted them. The parallel that Sor María draws between herself and the biblical prophets shows that she perceived her psychological kinship with those writers, canonical in her time but at odds with their own society. Her persona has much in common with that of Isaiah, whom she often quotes.

An equally biblical and highly visible element in Sor María's narratives is her choice of heavenly personages to act as the narrator. In one episode, God the Father, from his omniscient point of view, recounts the Prince of Darkness's rebellion and his insidious machinations against Sor María's purity, of which not even she has been fully aware. The claim that she has received such supernatural communication accomplishes more than one literary function.

Arenal and Schlau observe that many writing nuns appealed to divine inspiration and command to authorize their daring and to relieve what has been called their "anxiety of authorship."[10] For many of Sor María's readers, it has, of course, lent importance to her writings and also to her as a person for being worthy of such an honor. More complex is the way it allows Sor María to present an assertive self-image. An analytic but impatient reader might accuse her of a recurrent, clumsy expression of false modesty, but that would be an oversimplification.

On reaching the end of the passage narrated by God, Sor María feels an impulse to justify having included it and explains: "I have not wanted to leave out the Lord's words, which show my sins in the worst possible light, for they deserved such a punishment, and the Lord's kindness in saving me from these dangers." On the surface of the text, the image remains intact of a humble author who is merely a tool without any value of her own, an image that is in tension with the prologue's parallels between her, the Virgin, and Jesus. Religious writings of the period stressed, paradoxically, that the Virgin rose so high because she so abased herself.

In writing about herself much as though she were the Virgin, Sor María was working through the problem of finding a discourse that would allow her to reflect accurately the split in her own feelings, so prominent in her autobiography, between self-worth (understood as not her own but as a favor to her from God) and self-scorn (internalized at some level from religious and social tradition). The effect of including the long passage spoken by God is entirely the opposite of what Sor María claims. Far from emphasizing her faults, it permits her to describe her suffering and her noble steadfastness without bragging but with hyperbole that does justice to the intensity of her feelings.

If we accept the idea that in this way Sor María externalized and expanded on her feelings about herself through the voice of God, several other phrases can be found that are less structurally developed but equally indicative of a tendency to focus on parts of her own personality and endow them with an autonomous existence. It is, of course, a literary procedure as common as it is basic to many genres, a favorite technique of the Renaissance and Middle Ages, which gave birth to so many debates between heart and head, body and soul, and other entities incapable of independent action. When the personality of the writer is viewed in theological terms, the result is works of the style familiar to English readers through the example of *The Pilgrim's Progress*.

Allegory took on exceptional prominence in Spanish convent literature both as part of the tradition that produced the religious theater known as *autos sacramentales* (in which concepts such as sin, grace, and transubstantiation play characters as powerful as the sacraments), and as a fundamental means by which nuns identified their fears and aspirations with cosmic forces. Arenal and Schlau have observed that "in a sense, the nuns allegorized themselves as well as the religious virtues they were attempting to emulate or the vices they wished to avoid. They exerted themselves to live in the sensation of sharing Christ's life on earth and in heaven."[11]

In this vein, Sor María addresses her sufferings, then explores their meaning for her in a series of metaphors: "You happy trials, the gateway to Heaven . . . How can I ever recount the combat I endured? How the tribulations of my heart? How the cruel and furious waves?" From this mode of apostrophizing her feelings in a narrative about herself to the personification of self-affirmation in the protagonist of *The Mystical City of God* would be for her a single step, although admittedly a bold one.

This example illustrates another aspect of Sor María's writing, a stylistic trait toward which the late Renaissance (i.e., the second, Baroque half of the so-called Spanish Golden Age) evolved, that of richly supplying details for pictures, graphic or narrative, that the neoclassic Renaissance had insisted should be simpler so as to be unified clearly in message and organization. By incorporating all the details, the essential objective of intellectual modeling of complex reality was achieved, but the risk was that the unifying structure would get lost beneath the abundance of specific cases that were hung from and piled on top of it. Although undeniably full-bodied for twentieth-century tastes, Sor María's luxuriant language usually avoids that danger. While at times as thickly put on as oil paint with a knife, by and large her language gains impact and strength by a verbal unfolding of concepts that is typical of Calderón without falling into Góngora's labyrinthine obscurity, to compare her with two well-known writers from her time.

One of Sor María's favorite devices, which strikes the rushed sensibility of our age as repetitious, is drawing the borders of an idea by clustering nearly synonymous words. For example, she tells us that trials leave one's soul "strong and fit and experienced." Lucifer's challenge to Heaven is an "uncalled-for proclamation and daring threat." There is no doubt when Sor María tells the devil that "I detest, abominate, and confound you, declaring you anathema in the sea of your evil." Similar is Sor María's creation of forceful statements by putting together antithetical terms in a phrase with a paradoxical feel, in a manner typical of the Spanish Baroque: "I do not want to go on any more about these trials, although I could say a lot on this subject. I will say more about it through silence than by speaking, as can be gathered from what I have said."

The last technique on a curve of increasing complexity is the use of a series of rhetorical questions, graduated in intensity and length to produce an impressive climax. Witness Sor María's emphatic indignation at Satan's insolence toward God and the Virgin: "Why do the heavens not faint? Why do the creatures not help to avenge this insult? Why do the elements not run wild? And why do the seraphim not annihilate that power, undoing it along with its lying stories and false-hearted treacheries?"

Still, for all its Baroque complication on the level of sentence structure, Sor María's discourse has an undeniable appeal that comes from a straightforward simplicity in its exuberant description of her feelings and experiences. Like Spanish colonial art, it is Baroque gone naive. Immediate and uncalculated in its vision, it disarms and delights.

Manuscripts of "The Crucible of Trials"

The three manuscripts I consulted for the text of the two prologues are all eighteenth-century ones preserved in the National Library: F (MS 9417); MS 6057, which I call Q, for its old call number Q 257; and MS 848.[12] I have chosen the second as my base text, since it seems to have suffered from a minimum of scribal errors and editorial changes, but the relatively few discrepancies among the three point to a common source not far removed.

Text of "The Crucible of Trials"

How the Lord prepared me in the crucible of trials as a preamble to this infused knowing, and that it is necessary for the soul to be blind and dead to earthly things and their delights so that, not seeing their empty attractions, it can understand and see the divine ones.

As the heavens, the earth, and the Lord, whom I love and adore, are my witnesses, the favors granted by the Most High would not have satisfied me or filled the hollow in my heart if His Highness had not set me such a long, drawn-out preamble of trials. And earnestly I declare that this knowing and these mysteries cannot be seen except by eyes that have been thoroughly purified, for the soul that is to be the chosen vessel of infused knowing needs to pass many times through the crucible of trials and insults; for the sun of justice dazzles with its powerful rays all residents in this world who are not clean and purged of the dregs of earthly life. It is impossible for two contrary things to coexist in the same place, as is the case of darkness, the delights and pleasures that the world deceptively offers, with wisdom, special kindnesses, and infused knowing from the Most High, for his highness and his wisdom are not found in gold or silver, nor much less in those who are swollen with worldly pride. Generous and compassionate, the Most High has chosen to separate out and remove even the marrow of bones when it is contrary to his law and virtue, and with his double-edged sword to cull the bad seed from the good, placing some on the right and some on the left.

The Lord has given me many trials that no tongue can explain or enumerate; I would like to recount them, but it is impossible because it would be necessary to make many volumes of books. The Lord knows well from whose hands I have received them, and I have been as pleased and appreciative to have them as though I had received the greatest benefits and favors, for His Highness opened my eyes to the truth. And what is unquestionably true is that trials, when one is scorned and humiliated and in distress, are the path to find the highest knowledge and wisdom. What the Lord communicated to me came by that road, and they have not been trials for just a year or two, but a great number of them, ever since I reached the age of rational thought, and I can assure you this is no exaggeration.

It is all well known to He who has watched over my roads from my youth and who is with me in my tribulations and afflictions, first causing me pain, then giving me new vitality; He has given me as much snow as my wool could take. And the holy angels to whose care are entrusted my protection and defense, and who have accompanied me as my very own guardians, can vouch for this truth, for Their Highnesses have comforted and helped me take heart in life's shipwrecks, making me understand the excellence of my trials, that they are a precious pearl and rare gem, advising me to purchase them at any price. And what could be worth more to me than these trials? With them I bought a treasure more valuable than gold and just as rich and supreme, as I will recount later.

You happy trials, the gateway to Heaven, worth as much as all it contains. How can I ever recount the combat I endured? How the tribulations of my heart? How the cruel and furious waves? Sometimes it seemed that I wanted to sink down to the bottom, and others to rise up high to throw myself down more violently. Throughout my life, the author of all things strengthened me with illnesses, sadnesses, and despair. But I found comfort in the heights and the Lord's help. And my heart never delighted in earthly things, for they did not fill the emptiness in my spirit. For this reason, the world died for me in my youngest years, before I really came to know it.

And not only have I suffered these trials, which I could not exaggerate if I tried, but the Most High has chosen for me that all the kindnesses His Highness has done me have always been prepared and preceded by a preamble of afflictions and much pain. The fact is that we human creatures are incapable of responding to God's action unless we first walk the path of bitterness and trials, and though it is true that trials do not in themselves give blessings, they predispose. Suffering, pain, and bitterness are the little bundle of myrrh that my soul embraced and wore close to its heart.[13]

When it was the eve of some important and solemn day, I preferred first to endure pain and bitter suffering, then later as a consequence enjoying God's goodness in the form of joy and happiness. The Lord arranged this wisely and prudently to shape and fashion my raw nature, disciplining me like a judge to make my spirit strong and fit and experienced in its struggles. And He was thereby lavishing affection on me like a father who cares for me, loving me as though I were a little girl and a sister with flat breasts.

The Lord followed the same procedure in this matter of infused knowing; it is a fact that the Lord sent me more than eighty days without any comfort, encouragement, or kindness—I mean nothing as a special favor for me—for I did not see His Highness. For me, that was the greatest trial; I was deprived of the sight of Him. They were the greatest and most unbearable trials I have ever had, and although I have said something in a declaration of faith that I made while suffering them, I shall here briefly recount what I heard from the mouth of God Himself so as better to make myself clear using his own words, which contain much to think about. It is all very succinct, and I include it here as a preamble to what I am going to write; it tells what the Lord did to prepare me to receive infused knowing.

His Highness spoke to me after I had begged Him to show me the danger and trials I had undergone, and to my request, I had the following answer. Revealing the danger of my struggle, the Lord said to me, "My wife and turtledove, I am fully aware of your anxieties, as I have been during your struggle, and for that reason I wish to hear you acclaim Me when it is done, for your joyful affirmation is as sweet to Me as sonorous instruments. Well may you magnify Me after your struggle, for having kindly saved you from it and from your enemies, and you should understand how powerful they have been. Listen carefully, my wife. Twice the devil raised his head against my power, my omnipotence, the first in Heaven when, trusting in his weak strength, followed by his henchmen, he made himself a captain of outlaws and called himself the raging dragon.

"In vain he sought to match himself with his Creator, and making that uncalled-for proclamation and daring threat, said, 'I will ascend to Heaven; above the stars of God, I will set my throne on high; I will sit on the mount of assembly in the far north; I will ascend above the heights of the clouds; I will make myself like the Most High.'[14]

"Such was his extreme pride, and I punished him severely with the might of my powerful arm. Just a word spoken in my name was enough to hurl him into the depths, leaving him in the most miserable state one can imagine. His rage and anger grew against the power of my right hand, and since he once had seen himself so favored by it—and that was what most of all should have made him loyal—when he was punished, his pride grew, too, until he wanted to suck up the River Jordan. It grew so much that he sought for revenge.

"The second time he raised his head against me it was against mankind, since that is in my image. Then he attempted to knock mankind from the happy, fortunate state in which I had placed it and from which it finally fell. From that time on, he has turned furious, and since mankind has given him such a free hand and so he is at such an advantage over them, he harasses and upsets the whole world, which by its sins increases his chances to do harm. And so they have compelled me by their bad lives and evil doings to leave them vulnerable to his danger, their fortune in his hand. But moved by compassion, I have sent those same afflictions to those I love, thereby turning the

rod of my justice into that of Moses and with it doing acts of pity.[15]
One of the principal ones has been to make of them the preamble and
rigorous training necessary for the infused knowing I have shown and
communicated to you.

"In those more than eighty days during which you suffered, the
events were as follows. By lying words spoken into your mind to con-
vince you to sin, and by bodily visions and other sorts of lying stories
that hell invented and tried, they attempted to persuade you with
more than a thousand dangerous temptations. More than fifty times a
day all hell convoked an assembly and council meeting against you.
Indeed, it invented more and more tricks and diabolical arts to persuade you. And such evil temptations that I do not command you to
write them down, nor would it be possible or right to do so. I shall
only say, my wife and turtledove, that your trials have been the worst
anyone has endured and beyond the strength to endure of many people
added together.

"The pride of this terrible and ancient serpent was horrible, so great
that had I given him the chance, he would have torn you apart like a
violent, blood-thirsty beast and undone you. The strength of the sea
and its waves, no matter how furious and high they may be, or the
rapacious nature of the most violent beasts, or all the evils born from
the world—all of that is like throwing a drop of water into the sea in
comparison with the steadfast malevolence against you of the evil
serpent. It is impossible, dear soul, for you to understand how your
struggles have really been and how dangerous. If you fully understood
what you went through, your anxiety would be so intense that, unless
I relieved it supernaturally, your realization of the danger in which
you had been would make you unable to live even a quarter of an
hour. Reflect on these kindnesses of mine, which are great, and your
voice will cry out like a flame, for I want to hear your confession and
your praise. And consider, dear soul, that in fact the danger to you
was greater than I have indicated and that you reacted like the weak
creature you are, so your obligation to repay Me is even more, for I
have shown you special kindness, helping and protecting you in the
midst of your tribulations."

I have chosen not to leave out the words of the Lord, which show my sins at their worst, for they deserved such a punishment, and the Lord's kindness in saving me from such dangers; it has been his will for all this to happen. The Most High commands and orders me not to tell the temptations, and it is true some cannot be named, so that is what I will do. What I can definitely say is that there was no torture, no lying and made-up story, and no awful dread that the devil did not put to use against me, nor any fantasies he did not place before my eyes, nor any heresies to which he did not try to convert me, nor any affliction with which he did not disturb me, nor any acquaintance now deceased whose image he did not conjure up and show to me. Who could ever fully describe all the kinds of temptations, who the fearful and false visions he showed me, mixing his lies with the images of truth itself?

Oh, high mysteries of my unfathomable God, whom I love and who is the height of goodness! If Your Highness, my Lord, had not granted me the ability to see through the devil when he had hidden your truths, how would it have been possible for me, a miserable worm, to escape unharmed from the dragon's mouth? And finally, my God, and this is the strongest way I can describe it, the ancient serpent went so far (though he came to regret it) as to pretend deceitfully that he wanted to receive and do holy things, expecting and asking to be given holy water. Could he create a bigger lie than to give hell the appearance of Heaven, pretending to do miracles, the poisonous serpent turning himself into an angel of light, often impersonating the saints in images of them he placed before my eyes? And this Luciferic pride has gone so far as to loose his treacherous tongue against Heaven itself. And since the devil has gone so far as to raise his head against your divine majesty and your most holy mother, my lady, why do the heavens not faint? Why do the creatures not help to avenge this insult? Why do the elements not run wild? And why do the seraphim not annihilate that power, undoing it along with its lying stories and false-hearted treacheries? Oh, perverse evil! I detest, abominate, and confound you, declaring you anathema in the sea of your evil, and may you perish in it. I do not want to go on any more about these trials, although I could say a lot on this subject. I will say more about it through silence than by speaking, as can be gathered from what I have said. I think very highly of you, my trials, for you are the gateway to well-being, the means of reaching the Heavenly Jerusalem, and all true wealth. Unbelievably fortunate are the souls who possess it. Praised be the Lord forever, as He is by all the souls in glory. And since He placed us as travelers here below, we pray He place us among his chosen. Amen.

In the following chapter, I recount an incident that brings out the intensity of my trials and struggles, and above all the protection and generous compassion of the Most High, as the following will make clear.

Chapter 2

About a very special event in which I was involved, a big, dangerous fight where the protection and help of the Most High shone brightly, defending me and strengthening my weakness so I might tread on my evil, bloodthirsty enemies.

After I had endured the fearful and intense trials that have been recounted, while I was wishing I might have some relief and comfort of the kind I often receive from the hands of the Most High, for . . . they come to the soul through his great compassion. It was getting worse, since for many days Heaven had been closed to me; during the whole time of my struggle, I had not seen either the Lord, or his angels, or any light at all. And this was the hardest one of all my trials, for that had not happened to me ever since the Lord called me so clearly, and not a day would go by without my seeing His Highness. The pain was breaking my heart, both from the anxiety that my own guilt might be responsible for this pain and from the absence of help and defense in so many trials. And the longing to possess what my soul lacked, which was the sight of Him, caused such a burning desire in me that I was like a wounded doe panting to come to the waters of grace.

After this long and drawn-out night, I longed for the happy dawn to break over my soul, for the sun of justice I had missed so much to shine upon me. My keen desire to see my beloved grew, and His Highness, who is never far from those who are troubled and hears all who earnestly call to Him, heard my voice, which from the depths of my being was calling out to Him. The sky grew calm, and I saw the happy star that brought me good news of the coming dawn, and the star became a most holy angel. The sight of it cheered me greatly for two reasons. First, because so many days had gone by without my seeing anything remarkable, in a vision, and secondly because in his appearance, I saw the same image I had formed in my mind of his Creator and my beloved, and that was the food with which my soul nourished itself; not with the sight of Him, but the image I saw reflected in the holy angel, who said to me the following:

"My dearest, wife of the Most High, listen carefully to my words, for I am the ambassador of the great King and his messenger. Take courage and draw comfort for your heart in the midst of your trials, for soon they will reach their end and that of your struggle. You will have one that will last for three days; it will be very violent and more dangerous than any ever heard of before. Draw comfort for your heart and strength for your arm, and truly defend the cause of the Most High. At the end of this fight, the Lord will be most generous with you, communicating his infused knowing, but He wants you to go through this fearful war and emerge victorious from it. The Lord will be your light and guide. Obey his word and will and in all ways be alert and careful in whatever may befall you."

After this notice, which was given to me on the day of the octave of the assumption of the Queen, it happened one night—while I was gravely ill, wasted away, and debilitated—that I saw an angel, and he greeted me, saying, "The Lord be your light and eternal well-being. Obey his command and will promptly and energetically." I replied, "Let his will be done in me, his handmaiden and slave." And then I saw that an angel was going to stay in my place in the infirmary (and it was my guardian angel), which is where I was during my illness.

I was taken or transported to another place; to better verify the truth of this, I observed the weather in the places where I was, and it was sometimes hot and sometimes cold. I also made out that I was going down into the earth and through some caverns. After many dark paths and caverns, I reached a very large one; out of it was leaping a terrible, powerful fire, very thick, blue and black in color. As I was standing there, out came a motley crowd of devils whose looks were frightening and horrible, and one, who especially stood out, sat down on a rock that was there in this cavern, while all the others remained standing and so showed their lesser station.

This is as far as the original went from which this copy was made; as the vision that it is describing is left unfinished, it is suggested that some other copy be looked for to supply what is missing so it can be copied and this work not be left incomplete.[16]

6

The Empowered Spirit

Childhood Remembered

"The Crucible of Trials," Sor María's bilocation to the Southwest, and *Face of the Earth* reveal much about Sor María's adolescence and early womanhood. They make clearer the development in those years of her imagination and worldview that culminated in *The Mystical City of God*. But what of her childhood, when her personality was formed? Sor María, too, asked that, and in her unfinished autobiography she tried to sort out—from the perspective at the end of an extraordinarily active life of the imagination—what her earliest memories were and what they meant for her later concepts of God, the world, and herself.

The reader of Sor María's reconstruction and analysis of her first years (published thirty years ago in Spanish as an appendix to Seco Serrano's edition of her correspondence with the king) does not have to accept any specific psychological interpretation of mysticism, or even Sor María's own interpretation, to see the relevance of those memories to her writings. Two or three things become apparent immediately. First, as Sor María goes back in time as far as possible, she recalls an authoritarian personality that strongly impressed her by its power and moral supremacy relative to her own weakness and tendency to commit improper acts. Interpreting it as a heavenly father, as Sor María does, this creates in her a strong awareness of the power and knowledge of God, Creator of all the incomprehensible objects and energies that surround and affect her, a God that has been offended by the innately sinful nature she senses within herself. The anguish she re-creates in the autobiography is truly that of a little child, anxious at her inability to assure the granting of the basics needed for life:

> His invincible Majesty showed me within myself the aspects and prop-
> erties of my nature and that of all rational creatures, but it does not seem
> that is what we are, for if we were, we would die of fear of ourselves; I
> realized something that is beyond my power to express, and I perceived
> something that with all the terms we use put together is still impossible
> to explain. I saw myself so reduced to nothing that I could not see what
> to look at, and I perceived that ever since the Most High had in his
> kindness seen fit to give me being, life, and compassion, He had from
> me nothing but ingratitude for the benefits I received from the Lord's
> hand. . . . These two contrary extremes the Most High showed to me,
> extremes of good and evil, light and darkness, grace and sin, affected my
> spirit. With astonishment, fright, and unrest, I wept; I was anxious
> whether I would obtain the good of which I was aware and flee the evil
> threatening me; I perceived that by myself alone, I was unable to achieve
> grace, though not to lose it and commit sins. Since the fragility of my
> nature, my miserable and afflicted state, were so firmly implanted
> among my ideas and in my heart, my pain and suffering grew and grew;
> I developed such a fear that I have never lost it, rather it has steadily
> increased, as I wonder whether I shall offend God and lose grace with all
> the countless good things that go with it; I turned to that Lord that I had
> seen and known to be the cause of all causes, the origin, beginning, and
> author of every perfect gift; I dwelt on my memories of his fair beauty,
> gentleness, mildness, and greatness, and like a very little child would say
> to Him: "My Most High Lord, do not go away from me, do not separate
> me from You, give me your hand so I may have You and not be left alone;
> grant me the goodness of the grace You have shown me and take from
> me the great evil of the sin I have known."[1]

Such despair at one's own sinfulness and helplessness is so common in the intensely spiritual that the saint Juan de la Cruz, close friend of Teresa de Avila, classified it as a usual stage on the path to mystic union with God.[2] Sor María, like many young mystics, felt she had no merit in herself, that unless given forgiveness and special help, she would be lost and miserable, unable to win mercy from the heavenly father and judge. Similarly, reassurance regarding her worth is the theme of most of Christ's communications to Kempe,[3] who made efforts to confess and be given absolution as often as possible as a way of allaying her fears.[4]

Feminist scholars who, like Weber, have analyzed the rhetoric of women's mystical writing in the context of Counter-Reformation Spain have stressed the empowering aspect of discourse that gives lip service to the norms of male dominance but only as a vehicle to female authorship. But others, like Warner, have made the point that Catholicism's misogynistic strain has created anxieties in Catholic women about their own worth that have been difficult to overcome except by accepting the consolations and partial reassurances that, along with reduced status, the church concedes them, and that, in general, anthropology finds religion often creates fears so as to render itself necessary in their alleviation.[5] Sandra McEntire, in a recent study of compunction in the Middle Ages, observes that in spite of the morbid impression on modern readers, a focus on weeping and personal sinfulness was an ancient aspect of Christianity that took on special importance as the Middle Ages grew to a close.[6] The guilt of sinners for having put Jesus through the agonies of the cross to redeem them was keenly felt in the fourteenth century and beyond. In sum, anyone capable of imagining and writing as intensely about feminine heroics as Sor María did clearly was not lacking in self-esteem; yet to maintain that she did not need a psychological as well as a rhetorical strategy to escape from the bonds of patriarchal views of women that undermined her childhood seems to presuppose an almost superhuman level of self-confidence.

From a conviction of powerlessness, then, in the psychological presence of what has come to be known as learned helplessness, no heroic self-creation such as demonstrated by Kempe, Teresa de Avila, and Sor María would seem possible, yet each woman found a way. To Kempe, there came a vision in which Christ sat on her bedside and reproached her for insufficient love. Thereafter, she resolutely followed her convictions in spite of conflicts with the church that included talk of her as a heretic.[7] For Teresa de Avila, liberation came in her discovery of a new way to understand humility, the virtue insistently preached to women and thought of as a prime requisite for anyone committed to a life of inner prayer. In this solution, she was helped by other mystic writers of her time who stressed that one must have confidence of being worth enough to receive God's loving favors. To close oneself to God's power to transform human life and make it more noble was to commit the sin of despair and false humility.[8]

For Sor María, the Virgin, much more than Christ, would become the medium of her transformation. Mary came to be the comforting Mother within, who was able to supply Sor María with the wisdom and strength the Father demanded. A related, centuries-old practice, even within the predominantly patriarchal church, is to pray to Mary to intercede for sinners with the judge of the world. The same impulse manifested itself in the writings of Teresa de Avila, Juan de la Cruz, and many nuns from the late Middle Ages through the seventeenth century[9] in the transference of feminine properties to a usually masculine god. God's comfort and nurturing love, for example, when contrasted with God's strict judgment, were compared to a mother's milk in an image that showed the divinity as both maternal and paternal. In *The Dark Night of the Soul*, Juan de la Cruz writes: "With no effort on the soul's part, this grace causes it to taste sweet and delectable milk and to experience intense satisfaction in the performance of spiritual exercises, because God is handing the breast of His tender love to the soul, just as if it were a delicate child."[10]

The second principal idea that emerges from Sor María's autobiography, and it defines the direction her inner life had moved in the course of her life, is awe for the overwhelming properties of the Father, but carried to the point of empowerment, to being convinced that she herself is allowed to participate, to some degree, in those same sources of happiness. The attributes of God that most impressed Sor María were his power and knowledge. As mentioned in the opening chapter, Solaguren has pointed out her constant use of titles such as "the Almighty" and "the Most High."[11]

Sor María's attraction to knowledge, her desire to share in the power wrapped up in the secrets of the Ruler of the Universe, is expressed eloquently in her defense of the truth:

> Through the kindness of the generous and loving mercy of the Most High, the light of the Lord, coming out to meet me as I entered life through the door of rational thought, showed me the beauty and importance of truth so that I might love it and by that love be urged on to reach it. . . .

Another seven years and all my life I worked for the fertile Leah of humility, for the more the human creature delves deeply into the earth of self-knowledge, the greater is her fertility and more abundant the fruit she gives, for God raises up those who humble themselves. While He keeps his secrets hidden from the proud, He reveals them to the little people, giving them light and grace so that they may bring forth the fruits of eternal life.[12]

In comparing religions from all parts of the world, Mircea Eliade has concluded that force—the power and knowledge to create and sustain—is an essential part of the concept of the divine: "Evidently, for the archaic mentality, reality manifests itself as force, effectiveness, and duration. Hence the outstanding reality is the sacred; for only the sacred *is* in an absolute fashion, acts effectively, creates things and makes them endure."[13]

But although dazzled and frightened by the being who invented and governs the incomprehensible diversity of the universe, Sor María came to believe that He was not always distant and severe. The reason for that consoling and life-giving change in her emotional life, aside from God's maternal, milky kindness, she felt to be her willingness to suffer, to sacrifice herself as a martyred missionary, as a teenage girl who renounced the world in obedience to her stern parents' wishes. Her suffering in all her anxieties and other trials, as she saw it, had been relieved and rewarded, for she was favored with God's special love and confidence. Similarly, in *The Mystical City of God*, the Virgin is elevated to a position of extraordinary favor with God, who invests her with knowledge of and power over all things in preparation for her marriage to Him.

Luis de Granada and the Midrash

In addition to Teresa de Avila, whose famous *Life* probably influenced Sor María to undertake her own autobiography as part of her final, unfinished project of rounding out and polishing her collected works, there is another Spanish mystic whose writings Sor María likely knew and was guided by in conceiving the idea of writing the "autobiography" of the Virgin. In 1986 I was given special permission to enter, accompanied by two priests, the cloistered convent at Agreda to look through the manuscripts preserved there, and at that time, I also was able to examine the community's collection of books. Judging by the dates of the editions, many of the volumes may have been there from Sor María's time; in one volume, there were marginal notes that seemed to one of the coeditors of *The Mystical City of God* to be in Sor María's own hand. The two writers most frequently represented in that library, by far, were Teresa de Avila and Luis de Granada. The latter, even though long recognized as an author whom many of the best-known Spanish mystics read, particularly Teresa de Avila herself,[14] came as something of a surprise, for his name had not been connected with Sor María's. However, a review of his works shows a literary drift that makes the genesis of *The Mystical City of God* substantially easier to envision.

Although more of an ascetic than a mystic, Luis de Granada was explicit about the fact that God grants extraordinary knowledge to his beloved.[15] More specifically similar to Sor María is how he emphasizes that God, since he encompasses all things, can communicate the sight, sound, smell, taste, or touch of any part of the Creation, and does so for the delight of the elect in Heaven.[16] He thereby becomes a "mirror," just as Sor María repeatedly reports that the infused knowing she experiences reaches her when God chooses to act as a "voluntary mirror." The mirror was a favorite emblem of the Renaissance, usually signifying a model that should be emulated, but also, as in Saint Bonaventure, the belief that the visible world reflected its Creator.[17] The basically Platonic concept of models or ideas existing in a separate place, later identified with the Christian Heaven, made it an easy jump to the notion that God contained all things and could Himself act as a mirror or screen to make them visible apart from their familiar existence within the natural world.

That the data God mirrors for Sor María should include the intimate biography of the Virgin seems less strange when one knows, too, that Luis de Granada wrote "memorials" of Jesus' life based on details found in the gospel accounts, the apocryphal gospels, and traditions such as the joys and sorrows of the Virgin associated with the rosary.[18] While he seems to have added little of his own to these sources, Sor María's greater creative liberties may have been suggested, even urged upon her, by a reading of Granada's calls for the reader to imagine the state of mind, the thoughts and feelings, of Jesus, God, and the Virgin. He addresses the Virgin at some length, rhetorically asking how she felt while mothering the Son of God.[19] Although she does not reply in Granada's narrative, such information is at the heart of *The Mystical City of God*, in which the Virgin speaks to Sor María at the end of each chapter by way of commentary on the events. Not surprisingly, this homiletic element also is present in Granada's text, although he, in his office as author and preacher, more traditionally offers exegesis and exhortation. Another example is Pedro Malón de Chaide's *Book of the Conversion of Mary Magdalene*, written in 1588, which is a paraphrase of gospel accounts of the life of the protagonist accompanied by mystical poetry. The author was an Augustinian religious and university professor, a disciple of Luis de León.

In essence, Luis de Granada, Sor María, and Pedro Malón offer the reader historical novels whose characters are biblical figures. Edward Wilson, in comparing Spanish and English literature from the period, has observed that novelized books of devotion were largely absent in England but common in Spain.[20] Devotional literature, however, was not scarce in Kempe's time. Recent studies show that in late-medieval England, more lay people than members of religious orders owned the works of mystics such as Rolle, Hilton, and Julian of Norwich. Susan Dickman points out that a Franciscan manual of meditation on the life of Christ was one of the most popular books in England at the end of the fourteenth century.[21] In addition, there was a complementary basis in devotional practices for a novelistic use of the religious imagination. T. W. Coleman observes that "all devout believers were taught in their meditations to use concrete images; to select some incident in the life of Christ—particularly His Passion—and to think about it in such a realistic way as to make them feel they were present. That would be Kempe's method. To help her imagination she would seize on objects about her."[22] Kempe did retell central New Testament events like the Crucifixion and the birth of Jesus, even casting herself in minor roles such as arranging for lodging at the inn in Bethlehem. She tells us, for example, that when the Virgin was pregnant, she herself went "forth with Our Lady and with Joseph, bearing with her a pottle of wine and honey, and spices thereto." Later, "when Jesus was born, she provided bedding for Our Lady to lie in with her Blessed Son. Later she begged meat for Our Lady and her Blessed Child, and she swathed Him with bitter tears of compassion. . . ."[23]

Yet, curiously, such narrative kernels carried through to completion as full texts are largely absent in seventeenth-century England, and as with the rejection of the cult of the Virgin and the saints, one suspects the no-nonsense influence of the Reformation. The Franciscan enthusiasm of the late Middle Ages in England, France, and Italy lived on in Spain for reasons touched on in the first chapter. The Cistercians (with the inspiration of the Virgin's passionate troubadour, Saint Bernard) and the Franciscans had focused attention in Latin and, especially, vernacular texts on the humanity of Christ and his mother. In fact, from the second century onward, tales of the Virgin's life and death circulated in the Near East, the most influential being the apocryphal gospel of Saint James. From the beginning of the twelfth century, returning crusaders brought back to western Europe more samples of such narratives. Nativity tableaux, hymns focused on the Virgin's suffering at the crucifixion, and the emerging church theater all dramatized and encouraged the sort of imaginative intimacy with the lives of the holy family that we encounter in *The Mystical City of God*.

In short, there would seem little need to look beyond this tradition to explain why this genre flourished in Spain when it did not in England. Yet once again there are indications that the specific character of such works in Spain reflects a fusion of the Christian tradition of expanded biblical narrative with the Jewish one. Jewish elements are pronounced in the writings of Luis de León, and Swietlicki has found evidence for Christianized cabala in the work of Luis de Granada.[24] Cabala, moreover, has much in common with another Jewish intellectual legacy, the midrash, which Rabbi Moshe Weissman has explained in traditional terms: "The Almighty dictated to Moshe the text of the entire Torah. . . . At the same time, he provided Moshe with a detailed Oral Explanation of the text which He was dictating. The Written Text of the Torah constituted mere notes, brief allusions to the elaborate Oral Torah. . . . Moshe and the Sages who followed him carefully preserved not only the written Torah-scroll but also the Oral Explanation thereof. . . . They studied it and transmitted it from one generation to the next."[25]

The oral "explanation" of the biblical five books of Moses, and later all of the Hebrew Holy Scriptures, can be thought of as divided into two parts, one mystical/magical and the other literary. The former, the cabala, was centered on secret messages and formulas intended by God for the illumination of the wise, often encoded in the numerical values assigned to Hebrew letters.

Some cabalists, hoping to use such secrets for their own purposes, actively sought to decode the biblical text, whereas mystics like Sor María awaited God's illumination to learn more about divine intentions. Jorge Luis Borges' short story "Death and the Compass" describes a detective's search for a cabalist who, he mistakenly believes, is committing murders in order to discover the lost pronunciation of God's name and thereby gain immense power. The Italian Renaissance humanist Pico della Mirandola, himself engaged in the search for occult connections to the forces that drive the universe, "held that Pythagoras, Plato, Aristotle, Jesus, Saint Paul, and Dionysius the Areopagite were all privy to the secret, unwritten Cabalistic doctrine of Moses."[26] Cabala also developed a complex angelology and demonology. There is general agreement by historians of English literature that Milton's presentation of devil personality and society in *Paradise Lost* was shaped by the writings of Robert Fludd, an English Christian cabalist, just as Sor María's conception of her six guardian angels derives from Spanish cabala.

The literary side of the unwritten Hebrew Bible is known as the midrash. Like Sor María in *The Mystical City of God*, the midrash provides the details missing in biblical narrative. For example, it explains what was in God's mind when He commanded Abraham to sacrifice his son, and it supplies the dialogue surrounding the event. The midrash also is similar to Sor María's work in that it draws not only on written sources but on folklore and popular legends as well. Midrashic accounts figure prominently in Luis de León's glosses on the Song of Solomon and Job.[27] In this cultural context, works like *The Conversion of Mary Magdalene* and *The Mystical City of God* seem almost as Jewish as they do pre-Reformation Catholic.

The Virgin as Role Model

As in all fiction, the characters in *The Mystical City of God*, aside from the universal truth they may offer us, spring from the personality of the writer. From a literary historian's point of view, the Virgin whom Sor María describes is unquestionably a self-projection, a liberated alter ego, while the panoramic story is her imaginative, spiritual view of herself and her place in the world.

Sor María, of course, approached the Virgin from the point of view of shaping her own life by imitation, feeling that she acquired the qualities and powers of her model. But as Eliade points out, within Christian tradition, Jesus, not Mary, usually has been the model: "This Christian love is consecrated by the example of Jesus. Its actual practice annuls the sin of the human condition and makes man divine. He who believes in Jesus can do what He did; his limitations and impotence are abolished. 'He that believeth on me, the works that I do shall he do also. . . . ' (John 14:12)."[28]

As for similarities between Sor María and the Virgin, the list is extensive. Suffice it to say that both are mystics and experience the same types of visions; both are impersonated by angels when temporarily called away to Heaven or other parts of the world to spread the gospel; both are abbesses, the Virgin having founded the first convent, later accepting the post at Sor María's convent, and then delegating the responsibility back to her; and they are alike in details such as being vegetarians and prostrating themselves on the floor in the form of the cross to pray.

The question of Sor María's view of herself and her place in the world is raised especially by the nine chapters that open the third book and describe the preparations made for the Virgin's marriage in Heaven to God the Father immediately before the consummation of the Incarnation.[29] The nine chapters correspond to nine days, which are called a novena celebrated by the Trinity, and on each day God mirrors for her in visions a ninth part of all knowledge, of all that can be known by any being except God. The first six days are patterned on the creation of the world, the subject matter for each day corresponding to what was created, plus some additional theological matter. For example, on the first day, the Virgin learns facts such as the dimensions of the heavens and earth and how they were created, the nature of the angels, and much more. To this is added an understanding of why God, self-sufficient and self-glorious, chose to create the universe. By the time of her wedding, the Virgin shares in a large part of God's omniscience. To complement her knowledge, God also gives her power, with which she may command not only the angels, as Queen of Heaven, but the earth as well, and all that exists, animate and inanimate. Yet her response is always the same: renewed humility and a petition that God take human form and redeem the world.

This concept, a belief in the Virgin acquiring comprehensive knowledge prior to marrying God, though striking, is not found only in the work of Sor María de Agreda. Moreover, there are partial parallels in other mystics to the symbols and narrative situation she has made use of. As part of the tradition of the church's symbolic reading of the Song of Solomon, nuns, of course, marry Jesus, and Teresa de Avila, like many Christian mystics, used the analogy in a mystical sense.[30] Teresa de Avila also speaks of a preliminary stage of spiritual development as a betrothal, a metaphor that also becomes an episode in *The Mystical City of God*,[31] one similar in structure to the wedding but greatly simplified. The same biblical book read mystically was the model used by Juan de la Cruz in his *Spiritual Canticle*. In *The Mystical City of God*, the Song of Solomon is visibly present in phrases drawn from it and woven into Sor María's text,[32] as well as in an idea that governs the entire nine chapters: like the bride in the Hebrew epithalamium, the Virgin wins the heart and stirs the desire of God by her beauty, but it is a spiritual beauty, a beauty that grows and becomes ever more irresistibly attractive in God's eyes as time after time she responds to his gifts of knowledge and power with renewed humility and pleas for the salvation of the world.

Kempe's description of her own marriage to God is part of a less allegorical current within the tradition, one closer to the sensual emphasis of the pre-Christian text but, characteristically, drawn less from literary sources than from daily experience. The reader feels present at a homey English wedding on learning that the guests, who were the Virgin, Christ, the twelve apostles, Saint Catherine, Saint Margaret, "and many other saints and holy virgins," wished the bride and groom "much joy together." The erotic associations of mystical union are suggested by the mention of the bride's pleasures, which illustrate well the physical nature of her visions: ". . . for she felt many great comforts, both ghostly comforts and bodily ones. Sometimes she felt sweet smells with her nose. They were sweeter, she thought, than ever was any sweet earthly thing that she smelt before. . . ."[33]

In Sor María's description of the Virgin's wedding, the book of Esther serves as the basis for a more theological orientation to the episode, present in an analogy between the Virgin and Esther, who found favor in the eyes of King Ahasuerus and saved her people while dressed in royal robes. In a tradition that includes the medieval mystic Catherine of Siena, virtues are the soul's beautiful wedding clothes in its marriage to God,[34] and the Virgin, having been transported to Heaven, is dressed in clothes emblematic of both her virtue and her new status as queen and wife. Sor María describes a scene of rejoicing at court reminiscent of Ahasuerus' great feast given in Esther's honor when she replaced Vashti, just as the Virgin replaced Eve as Queen of the Earth. Sor María compares the Virgin's intercession to bring about the coming of Christ to that of Esther on behalf of the Jewish people, and her overthrow of the devil to Esther's of Haman. And finally, it seems more than a co-incidence that Luis de Granada[35] compared Ahasuerus' feast to the pleasures God grants to his elect in Heaven, an analogy possibly famil-iar to Sor María and plausibly adapted by her for Marian purposes, just as she adapted Granada's concept of God as a mirror of the delights of this world for those same elect.

What is important for a feminist reading of *The Mystical City of God* is that it is not enough for Sor María that the Virgin wins God's favor and special love as his bride. She stresses equality for the Virgin with God; the Trinity conducted the celestial novena, she asserts, so that the mother and father of Christ might be as much alike as possible.[36] Here the deification of Mary implied by the doctrine of the Immaculate Con-ception becomes explicit. Juan de la Cruz had dared to affirm that God could communicate his full nature to a mystic, comparing God to the sun, and a human medium to a pane of glass that transmits his essence and eventually partakes of it: "And God will so communicate His su-pernatural being to it that it will appear to be God Himself and will possess all that God Himself has."[37] But Sor María, fully in harmony with the Marian worship of her century, dared to assert that it was a woman who had become equal to God the father.

While Luis de Granada, like Sor María, affirmed that God adorned his bride with virtues and graces so she might be a worthy mother for his son, he specifically excluded intellectual accomplishments on the grounds that women had no opportunity to develop the requisite mental abilities.[38] In this, he either ignored or chose to overlook a tradition in which women religious writers had recast Mary as a wise woman, a Christianized form of Greek Sophia or Athene, whom we encounter as Beatrice in *The Divine Comedy*. A belief, which appears in Sor María's text, had developed that attributed to the Virgin the composition of works including both the Creed and the Magnificat. Whereas Luis de Granada emphasizes that Christ is the ruler of all Creation, in *The Mystical City of God* it is the Virgin who assumes that role, and as the work progresses, she assumes more and more of Christ's traditional attributes; she preaches and performs miracles along with him during his life, and after the crucifixion, she ascends into Heaven and, through the merit of her vicarious participation in her son's passion, becomes co-Redeemer of the World. Kempe established a similar parallel between Christ's suffering and her own.[39]

Finally, in addition to becoming ruler of the Creation, Sor María's Virgin becomes its co-Maker through her role as missionary, in that all civilizing of wild countries reproduces God's forming of the ordered cosmos out of chaos. The Virgin's entry into the Godhead through a ritual modeled on the creation of the world confirms this aspect of her nature. Eliade points out that "it was in the name of Jesus Christ that the Spanish and Portuguese conquistadors took possession of the islands and continents that they had discovered and conquered. The setting up of the Cross was equivalent to a justification and to the consecration of the new country, to a 'new birth,' thus repeating baptism (act of Creation)."[40]

The fact that it is a woman who in Sor María's work comes to stand on equal footing with God reminds us that it was her mother who dominated the household. One hesitates to speculate about the personal origins of writings on a subject of such universal interest as woman as goddess, yet it is striking that it was Sor María's mother,

Catalina Arana, who in a dream was authorized from above to turn the family home into a convent and to have her husband, sons, and daughters all take Franciscan orders. That powerful, directive figure recalls two mythical female figures studied by Marie Louise von Franz: a wise old woman, or Earth goddess, and a pure young girl with magical powers who guide women in their life struggles.[41] Indeed, Sor María's view of the Virgin combines the two, for she describes her as both immensely old and wise, having existed since before Creation, and incomparably pure (the Immaculate Conception, of course, being the paramount doctrine of the book). I think the connecting link between the two figures, as Sor María's work makes more evident, is that they represent the two times—before and after—in the traditional pattern of women's lives when they are less subject to men's sexual desires.

The Virgin as the Holy City

There is one more Agredan symbol for the Virgin Mary that calls for explanation: the metaphor from the novel's title that defines the Virgin as "the mystical city of God." In the biblical book of Revelation, at the wedding feast of the lamb, the New Jerusalem, equated with the faithful who constitute the church, is described as the bride of Christ. The image was developed over the centuries and applied to the Virgin, so that by Sor María's time, it was common in Marian devotional literature to compare the Virgin, in which God lived both as Christ and in the person of the Holy Spirit, to a building, often Solomon's temple, or a city, the New Jerusalem.[42] For example, it is a recurring motif in Cervantes' "Christian romance," *Persiles and Sigismunda,* most fully expressed in the hymn sung by Feliciana de la Voz.[43]

In many religions, the sacred city is the link between Heaven and earth, where the human meets the divine. Moreover, it is the navel of the world, where creation takes place, and has existed in Heaven since the beginning of time. Its preexistence is reflected in the traditions surrounding Solomon's temple: "Thou gavest command to build a sanctuary in thy holy mountain, And an altar in the city of thy habitation, A copy of the holy tabernacle which thou preparedst aforehand from the beginning."[44] All of these qualities can be applied to the Virgin as pictured by Sor María. Her marriage to God reflects the union of Heaven and earth, allowing Jesus to be both man and God, as the celestial novena prior to the Incarnation makes clear. In a real sense, she is the navel of the world, for in bringing God into the world by means of the umbilical connection between her and her son, her body is the place where Creation has been renewed, for Christ is traditionally the second Adam, humanity perfected and reborn to the greater possibilities of life. Moreover, Sor María envisions the Virgin as she does the holy city as having existed since before the Creation of the universe.

The most important antecedent in the Bible to Sor María's use of this symbol is found in the Apocalypse: "And I John saw the holy city, New Jerusalem, coming down from God out of heaven, prepared as a bride adorned for her husband."[45] This verse from Saint John the Divine, who like Sor María wrote of having been carried up into Heaven, presents the same conjunction of three ideas that we find in Sor María's writings: mystic revelation, the faithful as brides of God, and the City of God. Although subsequently developed in medieval traditions, Sor María brought these ideas together centered on the Virgin in a remarkable affirmation of the feminine.

Mystical Liberation?

Sor María's portrait of the Virgin is radically different from the one contained in the Gospels. It is tempting to think that in assimilating and articulating the wealth of Marian traditions that compose it, while simultaneously creating through a lifetime of struggle a picture of herself as existing heroically in the world, Sor María achieved what could be called a mystical liberation. Yet some feminists have viewed such visionary women as obsessively religious. What good is a mystical liberation?

Only better than none at all, a tough-minded answer might be, but two other considerations come to mind. First, as Arenal and Schlau have shown in convincing detail, nuns who expressed themselves in writing, including writing about visions far removed from the reality of their severely limited day-to-day existence, rose in esteem, both their own and that of others. One chapter in Arenal and Schlau's study is dedicated to the Spanish peasant nun Isabel de Jesús (1586–1648). Their description of the effect of mysticism on her life summarizes much of what I have said about its empowering effect on Sor María:

> Mysticism had many functions for Isabel de Jesús. Her visions allowed her to sever herself from one kind of life and undertake another. Through the visions she educated herself. They also led to her increased status and power in the world and to enough interest in her story to demand its recording. Psychologically, mysticism was vital to Madre Isabel's survival. While she absorbed and internalized the culture that surrounded her, she created her own inner world in which despair was more manageable and joy more frequent. Her transforming imagination was her protection and salvation as both a child and an adult. Moreover, it enabled her to experience religious ecstasy. Her mystical life with Jesus offered recompense for suffering and allowed her to reshape her personal existence. Isabel de Jesús used her visions to overcome fear and gain self-confidence. As she developed trust in her inner life, there grew in her a sense of mission.[46]

The social level at which Isabel began was unquestionably much lower than Sor María's, yet there are parallels to Sor María's life. Circumstances were extraordinarily limiting and difficult as she found herself obliged to live out all her aspirations cloistered within the walls of a small town. Her early bilocation to the American Southwest brought not only fame and friendship with powerful people in the larger world, but inner consolation, transcendence of self-doubt, and the growth of a heroic self-image that made possible and sustained her mission to bring to the world the story of what a woman's life ideally might be. Like Teresa de Avila, she believed that Mary and Martha, who were understood as representing the contemplative and active lives, must walk hand in hand as sisters. Within the limits imposed by their society, it was a precept Teresa de Avila and Sor María followed energetically and successfully, as reformers, administrators, and outspoken critics to be reckoned with in both ecclesiastic and court politics. Kempe, too, lived in a religious environment in which spirituality was linked primarily to the contemplative life, yet her record also is not only of intense prayer, but also its fruit in movement and change. She did not write an abstract manual of mystical experience but instead left the narrative account of her simultaneous activity as a wife, mother, and community member in a commercial English town, activity that insistently, restlessly sought to discard passivity as the touchstone of a woman's religious vocation.[47]

A second reply to objections concerning mystical liberation might have to do with Miguel de Unamuno's assertion that the fictional Don Quixote, living on with great vitality in the readers of the novel, is much better known and loved than the once flesh-and-blood Cervantes. Similarly, it is Sor María's protagonist of her novel, the dynamic Queen of Heaven and Earth, who has moved people's lives for three hundred years.

The treatment of spirited women in the Hispanic novel often has merited the description of defeatist, if not misogynist, for strong heroines far too often come to a bad end involving death, humiliation, and marriage. *The Mystical City of God*, in contrast, presents a self-assured heroine who lives an active and perfectly executed life of highly visible achievement—with her husband's respectful cooperation. The story of the Virgin's role in the early church, in formulating the Creed and traveling around the Mediterranean to spread the faith, makes her more than the equal of Saint Paul, Saint James (whom she assists in Spain), or any of the other early church fathers. It is Sor María's "fictional" Virgin's inner life, her novelized self, that her readers primarily know and seek to identify with, and that breaks with the traditional model presented to women of the Virgin as only passively long-suffering.

A more general objection to a focus on the Virgin Mary has been expressed by Warner and others who have decried the harmful consequences of the Virgin Mary having been one of the most influential models for women in our culture. In this view, worship of the feminine principle in the figure of one extraordinary, deified woman has done more harm than good to real women's circumstances, and respect for the feminine as an abstract often bears no relation to better treatment of women by men. Similarly, the invention of courtly love in twelfth-century Provence, concurrent with Saint Bernard's outpouring of awe-filled worship of the Virgin, is not regarded as a positive change in social attitude. The idealized and imaginary fair ladies (shaped more by male fantasy or flattery than by the social realities of Cathar egalitarianism, absent crusaders, and valued female heiresses with time for culture) make real women seem not more noble but deficient and undeserving by comparison. Indeed, when the Virgin is thought of, as she often has been, as a rigorously, marvelously pure, asexual person—yet one whose primary function is childbearing—she creates a role for women tied not only to the home but to severely contradictory feelings regarding their sexuality.

This is a charge whose truth must be conceded, and in the best of all worlds, the image of a different, more human, yet still admirable woman could and would be implanted within our society. But in the world that we feel the need to transform, goddesses do not die quickly, if at all. The Virgin will be with us for centuries to come. The pragmatic question is, what will she represent?

Should we doubt that she can change, we need only look at her ancestry. From the Near East, she absorbed the Egyptian Isis's maternal compassion as well as the Hebrew prophets' concern for the miserable, while from Greece she took on Athene's role as protector of communities and source of militant wisdom, combining them in a way that moved and inspired emerging Christian society. The transformation, and the energy it generated, were of the same magnitude as those of the early church's remaking of the winter solstice into a similar but more human festival of light, and the spring equinox into a more personal celebration of rebirth. Should our doubt persist, we must stretch out our hand and place it in the wound in the side of the Catholic church. In one part of the church, at least in some countries, feminist theologians like Uta Ranke-Heinemann are beginning to win the struggle with traditionalist prelates over the secondary role permitted to women by a hierarchy defined by masculinity and celibacy. In another part of the church, even within the centuries-old current of idealization, the movement toward theological equality for Christ and his mother continues. There is growing emphasis on her active consent in making the Incarnation possible, and conversations with those in touch with the Vatican affirm that the doctrine of her co-redemption of the world will be the next new dogma that Rome will proclaim. And finally, a substantial number of American Catholics are turning to what they dare to call the cosmos and a lovingly maternal presence felt to inform it, a presence whose contemplation they have rediscovered in the mass to the Virgin Mary. Like the popular theologian and preacher Matthew Fox,[48] they are seeking to restore the emotional in-

tensity of their faith, to find spiritual wholeness in right-brain synthesis as well as left-brain analysis, to reach across the chasm separating
science and religion, and to situate themselves within a more solidly
grounded universe than science's hypothetical construct governed by
pure chance. It is as part of all these historic movements that the active, undaunted, and sovereign protagonist of *The Mystical City of God*
speaks not only for the woman who transformed her own life in creating her, but to our own time as well.

Notes

Chapter 1

1. From Sor María's autobiography, in Seco Serrano, *Cartas*, 109:230. All translations from this and other works are mine unless otherwise noted.

2. See the thorough bibliographic study by Pérez Rioja, *Proyección*, with attention to the Agredist polemic on pp. 1–4.

3. Warner, *Alone of All Her Sex*, p. 240.

4. Ibid., p. 249.

5. Ibid.

6. Ibid., p. 247.

7. Ibid., p. 295.

8. From Pardo Bazán, *San Francisco de Asís*, cited by Serrano y Sanz, *Apuntes*, 1:575–76.

9. Serrano y Sanz, *Apuntes*, 1:576.

10. Giles, *Book of Prayer*, p. 49.

11. From Pardo Bazán, *San Francisco de Asís*, cited by Serrano y Sanz, *Apuntes*, 1:575–76.

12. María José Conde of the Universidad de León examines in more detail the portrayal of classic mysticism in modern Spanish novels in her unpublished paper, "La M. Patrocinio de las Llagas en la literatura española contemporánea."

13. Arenal and Schlau, *Untold Sisters*, p. 2.

14. Arenal, "The Convent as Catalyst," p. 149.

15. Arenal, "This life within me won't keep still," p. 158.

16. Arenal, "The Convent as Catalyst," p. 167.

17. Arenal, "This life within me won't keep still," p. 160.

18. Arenal, "The Convent as Catalyst," p. 167.

19. Holbrook, "Margery Kempe," p. 34.
20. Coleman, *English Mystics*, p. 157.
21. Arenal and Schlau, *Untold Sisters*, p. 9.
22. Weber, *Teresa of Avila*, p. 11.
23. Ibid., p. 15.
24. Pérez Villanueva, *Felipe IV*, p. 12.
25. Ibid., p. 71.
26. Ibid., p. 110.

Chapter 2

1. López Piñero, *Ciencia y técnica*, p. 70.
2. Arenal and Schlau, *Untold Sisters*, p. 131.
3. Ibid., p. 4.
4. López Piñero's study reviews in detail the history of the polemic.
5. Duhem, *Histoire des doctrines cosmologiques*, 3:8.
6. López Piñero, *Ciencia y técnica*, p. 213.
7. On Apianus' influence, see the monographic study by Ortroy, *Bibliographie de l'oeuvre de Pierre Apian*.
8. Agustine, *La ciudad de Dios*, 1:213.
9. Isidoro, *Etimologías*, 2:49.
10. For Cervantes' interest in the literary theory of the "legitimate marvelous," see Forcione, *Aristotle, Cervantes and the Persiles*.
11. Apiano, *Libro de la cosmografía*, p. viii.
12. López Piñero, *Ciencia y técnica*, p. 184.
13. Ibid., p. 171.
14. Venegas, *Declaración*, chapter 25.
15. Medina, *Suma de cosmographía*, p. 493.
16. Duhem follows the development of the Franciscan tradition in detail. See *Histoire des doctrines cosmologiques*, 3:397–529.
17. Venegas, *Declaración*, chapter 2.
18. Calvert, "Osuna's Meditations," pp. 7–14.
19. Duhem, *Histoire des doctrines cosmologiques*, 3:289.
20. Clavius, *In Sphaeram*, p. 267.
21. Alphraganus, *Brevis Compilatio*, chapter 21.
22. Clavius, *In Sphaeram*, p. 270.
23. Venegas, *Declaración*, chapter 38; calculated not to the lower surface of the sphere but to the midpoint of its thickness.
24. Ioannis de Toledo, *Cursos*, p. 105.
25. Serrano y Sanz, *Apuntes*, p. 578.

26. Seco Serrano, *Cartas*, 109:227.

27. Ibid.

28. Ibid., p. 225.

29. Ibid., p. 227.

30. Ibid., p. 224.

31. "In the name of the Most Holy Trinity, Father, Son and Holy Spirit . . . I am beginning to write as instructed, and there will be the following treatises: . . . . Fifth Treatise. The order of human nature that was made known to me when I was given the habit of knowing: the heavenly and elemental spheres, from the empyrion heaven to the center of the earth, and the most important things it contains; orienting it all to the knowledge and service of its Creator by means of useful doctrine." In Serrano y Sanz, *Apuntes*, 1:577.

32. See, for example, Serrano y Sanz, *Apuntes*, 1:596; Uribe, "Fondo Agredano," pp. 254–55; and Zarco Cuevas, *Catálogo*, 1:315.

33. Uribe, "Fondo Agredano," p. 256, no. 8.

34. Ibid., p. 260.

35. Arenal, "The Convent as Catalyst," p. 178.

36. Weber, *Teresa of Avila*, p. 109.

37. Márquez Villanueva, "Sobre la occidentalidad," pp. 135–68.

38. Márquez Villanueva, "Los inventos de San Juan."

39. Swietlicki, *Spanish Christian Cabala*, p. 29.

40. Giles, *Book of Prayer*, p. 66.

41. Weber, *Teresa of Avila*, pp. 21–23.

42. Dickman, *English Devotional Tradition*, p. 162.

43. Perry, *Moral Proverbs*, p. 9.

44. López Piñero, *Ciencia y técnica*, pp. 75–77.

45. Silverman, "Review," p. 70.

46. Swietlicki, *Spanish Christian Cabala*, p. 50.

47. McKendrick, *Woman and Society*, p. 41.

48. The discoveries by Peñalosa and Johnson are summarized in detail by Idalia Cordero Cuevas in *El "Buscón,"* pp. 89–103.

49. Pérez Villanueva, *Sor María y Felipe IV*, p. 395, no. 41.

50. Colahan and Weller, "An Angelic Epilogue," p. 58.

51. Pérez Villanueva, *Sor María y Felipe IV*, p. 63; Rossi, *Teresa de Avila*, p. 18.

52. Rossi, *Teresa de Avila*, p. 24.

53. Arenal and Schlau, *Untold Sisters*, p. 9.

54. Dickman, *English Devotional Tradition*, p. 167.

55. McKendrick, *Woman and Society*, p. 6.

56. Serrano y Sanz, *Apuntes*, 1:595–96.
57. Esteve-Barba, *Biblioteca de Toledo*, MS 288.
58. Uribe, "Fondo Agredano," p. 253.
59. Zarco Cuevas, *Catálogo de el Escorial*, 1:312; MS IV & 2.
60. It turns out to be paragraph 32. Statements made there by Samaniego tend to confirm the supposition of an early version and another polished one done in Sor María's last years:

After the death of a respected friar who was very devoted to the venerable Mother and a close confidant of Father fray Francisco Andrés, moved by that devotion and taking advantage of the opportunity that confidence offered, the latter copied for himself, although with the errors inevitable when it is done almost furtively, many of those early writings of hers, then saved them until his death; he collected them assiduously. After reading them he discussed their contents with the Servant of God, asking her what the facts were about them; so without any suggestion of idle curiosity he obtained detailed information about the stages in her inner life over the years. . . . Realizing what a service for the cause of Our Lord it would be, and how useful for others, for her to write her life . . . he obliged her to undertake it . . . . While engaged in that project death overtook her, cutting the thread of not only her life but also of her story. It will always sadden her readers that such a remarkable work was not completed, for the projected table of contents she made promised not only an account of the events of her life, which in themselves, especially when enriched by her intelligence and style, were most worth recounting, but also redone versions of all the treatises that had been destroyed by fire and which, moreover, would have been much improved, for at the end of her life her mind was more brilliant, eminent, and fertile.

Chapter 3

1. *learned and experienced*: From this point to the end of the paragraph, F has a variant reading: "Before and after this favor, I used to walk in the world and nourish myself with its elements and feed myself with the fruits it produces; I enjoyed them in every way but was in a deep sleep of ignorance, not recognizing in these indirect ways the Author of all things, failing to praise Him for providing them to me in such timely ways. Later His Highness removed these veils of forgetfulness and ignorance from my mind. All this moves me to praise, spurs me on to awaken lively feelings of love in my heart to praise the Creator of all things. How I wish that proclaiming what I have received were

an antidote for the harm that in this matter we mortals do ourselves, that my errors might teach and help correct others' understanding, for since it is infused knowing from the Lord, it must be for everyone—even though I express it here with such a stammering tongue."

2. *The will of His Highness be done*: Between these words and the phrase "my wife and turtledove," F inserts: "I was placed or carried (as it seemed to me) into the presence of the Most High, and while prostrate in obeisance, I heard His Highness say to me."

3. *dwelling*: The reading of F; A, in contrast, has the following nonsensical completion of the paragraph: "the earth is divided into four parts, which we inhabit."

4. *9,280 leagues*: the reading of A; F has "7,506 leagues."

5. *8,480 leagues*: the reading of A; F has "6,706 leagues."

6. *America*: at this point, A and F diverge for a considerable number of lines. The two versions take up similar themes, much more fully developed in F. The two coincide again beginning with the phrase, "Oh, most high, immortal King." Because there is so much more in F, I have reproduced it in the text. The version of A follows:

The world as a whole contains the number of leagues I have said, and in the center and heart of the earth are hell and purgatory and limbo, as I will say at the right time. The earth's thickness is 2,502 leagues, and halfway, which is in the middle, is hell, and to that point there are 1,251 leagues. Astonishing and most marvelous and remarkable is the immensity of this world so full of mountains, valleys, plains, and rough terrain, while others are very pleasant and have a great variety of plants, flowers, and fruits for an ungrateful mankind. Some parts of the world are uninhabitable, others not. Some parts of the global structure are densely populated by several different lineages, some Christians, others who are not and who do not know God because they flee from the light and the truth, while in other parts they call out to and value the Lord, and there is a diversity of very different peoples, while others are very much alone. In some places, there are Catholics who confess the faith, in others they scorn it, while other peoples do not know it. There is such a wide difference among peoples that it is impossible to name them all.

7. *the absolute tallest eight*: Isidoro referred back to Greek geographers on the subject of tall people: "It is told that in India there exists a people they call the mahrobioi, who measure twelve feet." *Etimologías* 2:51.

8. *half a yard high*: "the people the Greeks call Pygmies, because their stature is no more than a cubit." *Etimologías* 2:49.

9. *they reach the ground*: "It is told that in Scythia live the Panotians, with ears so big they cover up the whole body. In Greek *pan* means 'all' and *ota* 'ears'." *Etimologías* 2:51.

10. *Idolatry had its origin*: "There were also some powerful men, founders of cities, in whose honor, when they died, those who revered them erected statues to find some consolation in gazing on their likeness." *Etimologías* 1:719. Was it Sor María, who so identified with the mother of Jesus, that introduced the note of tenderness for a dead son?

11. *Nin*: King of the Assyrians, who descended from Assur and Shem, not Cain. *Etimologías* 1:713, 747.

12. *Bel, Baal, Balin, Belphegor*: "Bel is a Babylonian idol whose name means 'the old one.' He was known as Bel, father of Nin, first king of the Assyrians, whom some people call Saturn. With the name of Bel he was later worshipped among the Assyrians and the Africans, and for them in Phoenician Bal means 'god'. Among the Assyrians, due to one of their beliefs, he is called Bel, and also Saturn and Sun . . . Belphegor means 'image of shame.' It was a Moabite idol, known as Baal, on Mt. Phegor." *Etimologías* 1:723. Sor María summarizes and at the same time amplifies her source. For example, "Assyrians and Africans" becomes "some provinces," and a new form appears, *Balin*, alliteratively and rhythmically appropriate in the series. It seems to replace three words glossed by Isidoro but omitted in *Face of the Earth*: Belzebub, Belial, and Behemoth.

13. *The Memphians . . . mice*: "Among the Egyptians, Apis is the bull sacred to Seraphis, from which it takes its name. The Egyptians worshiped it as though it were a god, for it supplied them with omens. It would appear in Memphis. It was followed by one hundred priests who, suddenly, like lunatics, would begin to sing." *Etimologías* 1:735. Mendes was a city at the mouth of the Nile. *Lamiae* were boy-eating witches. Very likely made up since classical times are *Quipolitani*, "Who Citizens," and *Zinopolitani*, "Stranger Citizens." *Traodenses* is perhaps a misspelling of Trojans, who were the inhabitants of the Troad.

14. *Tanais River*: Now called the Don.

15. *Scythians*: A general term for the nomadic tribes of the north of Europe and Asia, beyond the Black Sea.

16. *Lake Maeotis*: The Sea of Azov.

17. *provinces*: Apianus used the word to mean Roman provinces, logically enough, since his geography is largely that of classical antiquity.

18. *the Ocean Sea*: Here the Atlantic, but all of the oceans, in contrast with the smaller seas, were thought of as forming one globe-encircling body of water called the Ocean Sea.

19. *Aquitania, Lugdunum, Belgium, and Narbo*: Aquitania was the southwest part of Gaul, Lugdunum the region around the modern city of Lyons, Belgium the north of Gaul, and Narbo the region around the modern city of Narbonne.

20. *Sarmatians*: Defined below as Lithuania, Poland, Wallachia, and Transylvania.

21. *Dania*: Denmark.

22. *the Chersonese*: Not to be confused with the Chersonese Peninsula in the Black Sea, the Chersonesus Cimbrica was the Latin name for Jutland.

23. *Vindelicia*: In southern Switzerland.

24. *Moravia*: In the Czech Republic.

25. *Pannonia*: Included parts of Austria, Hungary, and Yugoslavia.

26. *Moesia*: In Serbia and Bulgaria.

27. *Bohemia*: In the Czech Republic.

28. *Hercinian Forest*: Now known as the Bohemian Forest.

29. *Misna*: Apianus, in an index of cities, indicates this is the region containing Leipzig.

30. *Friesland*: In northern Netherlands and Germany.

31. *Silesia*: A region now in Poland and Czechoslovakia.

32. *the Mark*: the Mark of Brandenburg.

33. *Pomerania*: A region along the Baltic Sea, now in Germany and Poland.

34. *Wallachians*: Wallachia is now in Romania.

35. *Transylvanians*: Transylvania is in central Romania.

36. *Dacia*: A province north of the Danube corresponding roughly to Hungary, Moldavia, and Transylvania.

37. *Dalmatians*: Dalmatia was part of the former Yugoslavia.

38. *Illyrians*: Illyria corresponds in large part to Albania.

39. *Slavonia*: Basically Serbia.

40. *Gallia Togata*: An alternate Latin name for Cisalpine Gaul, i.e., the northern part of the Italian peninsula.

41. 1 Samuel 10:5–6.

42. A has no heading for chapter 7.

43. *Cetura*: Probably a scribal error; refers to Sarah.

44. *Ethiopian Sea*: Supposed by classical geography to lie to the south of Africa.

45. *the Mauritanias*: Corresponded to parts of Morocco and Algeria.

46. *Tangerine*: The western part of Mauritania, centered on Tangiers.

47. *Caesarean*: The eastern part of Mauritania, containing the town of Caesarea.

48. *Numidia*: Between Mauritania and the territory of Carthage; modern Algeria.

49. *Carthage, Byzacene, and Cyrene*: Carthage, now in Tunisia, was the westernmost, while Cyrene, bordering on Egypt, the easternmost.

50. *Pentapolis*: More accurately, Pentapolis was a district on the Libyan Sea, of the province of Cyrene.

51. *Mallow River*: Latin "Malva," now known as the Moulouya.

52. *Abila*: Now Mt. Acho at Ceuta, across the strait from Gibraltar.

53. *Ampsaga River*: In Algeria.

54. *Zeusis . . . Cato died*: Ancient cities with locations now in Tunisia.

55. *Hadrumetum*: Also in Tunisia, was the capital of Byzacene.

56. *Leptis*: The name of two cities on the North African coast. Leptis Magna was in Tripolitana and Leptis Minor in Tunisia.

57. *Cynips River*: Shown on Renaissance maps as the Cinyphus, it empties into the Mediterranean at the west end of Syrtis Major, in Libya.

58. *Tripolitana*: The district around Tripoli.

59. *Syrtis Major*: Syrtis was the name of two areas of sandy flats on the coast between Carthage and Cyrene. Syrtis Major was the shore of the Gulf of Sidra, while Syrtis Minor was along the Gulf of Gabes.

60. *Arae Philaenorum*: A frontier town of Cyrene, the southernmost point of Syrtis Major.

61. *Garamantes*: A tribe living in the Eastern Sahara.

62. *Catabathmos*: A tract of land in Libya between Egypt and Cyrene.

63. *Marmarica*: The region of Barkah in Libya.

64. *Arabia Petrea*: Classical geographers divided Arabia into Arabia Petrea, (for the city of Petra), Arabia Deserta, and Arabia Felix.

65. *Troglodytes*: A people of Ethiopia who lived in caves.

66. *Aegipanes*: A satyrlike people described by several classical authors; thought to be some kind of ape.

67. *Blemyes*: "It is believed that in Libya the Blemyes are born, who exhibit a headless torso and have mouth and eyes in the chest. There are others who, lacking a neck, have their eyes on their shoulders." Isidoro, *Etimologías*, 2:51. "Then toward the east there are people without heads, and who have their eyes on their backs, in the eastern mountains of India." Pliny, f.10v. I have translated from the Spanish Renaissance version by Hernández, *Historia natural*.

68. *Satyrs*: "Satyrs are little men with hooked noses, horns on the forehead

and hooves, like those of goats." Isidoro, *Etimologías* 2:51. "In a region called Catardul there are Satyrs, who are extremely fast; they run like animals, on all fours, but also standing erect, and they look like people; since they are so fast they can not be caught unless they are old or sick." Pliny, in Hernández, *Historia natural*, f.10v–11.

69. *big callous*: After these words, F adds "for they inherited it and everyone was born with it and now they all have one."

70. *Cynocephalians*: "The Cynocephalians owe their name to the fact they have dog heads; their bark alone makes it clear they are more animals than people. They are born in India." Isidoro, *Etimologías* 2:51. "In many other mountains there are people who have heads like dogs, dress in animal skins, and bark instead of speaking." Pliny, in Hernández, *Historia natural*, f. 10v.

71. *only one eye*: "In India are also engendered the cyclops, and they are called cyclops because they exhibit one eye in the middle of the forehead." Isidoro, *Etimologías*, 2:51. "They have only one eye in the forehead. They fight continually with the griffins for metal. Pliny recounts this, and he himself, supported by the authority of Herodotus and Aristeus, says that in a great valley of Mt. Imaus there is a region called Abarimon, in which there are some savage people who have their feet backwards, with the heel forward and the toes behind, who live together with the animals and are very fast. Not far from these live the Troglodytes, and next to them toward the west live some people without head or neck, having their eyes in their shoulders." Apiano, *Libro de la cosmografía*, f.46.

72. *pug noses*: "It has been written that in the far lands of the East there are races whose faces are monstrous; some have no nose, exhibiting a facial surface completely flat and without features." Isidoro, *Etimologías*, 2:51.

73. *one eye . . . literally*: "And if your eye causes you to sin, pluck it out; it is better for you to enter the kingdom of God with one eye than with two eyes to be thrown into hell." Mark 9:47.

74. *Monoculars*: The *monoculi* were a fabulous race of giants, each with but one leg (not "eye") of prodigious strength.

75. *unable to talk*: "They say that there are some who have no tongue and to communicate use only signs and gestures." Isidoro, *Etimologías*, 2:51. "Tauron writes that there are some savage peoples called Ceromandos, who have no speech, but make a terrible racket. Their bodies are covered with hair, their eyes green, their teeth like a dog's." Pliny, in Hernández, *Historia natural*, f.11.

76. *most holy*: the reading of F; A has "infinite."

77. *treasure*: the reading of F; A has "treasurer."

78. *Scythian Sea*: The reading of F; A has "Arctic Sea."

79. *Asia proper*: Asia was originally the name of a town in Lydia, a province corresponding to a part of Turkey that faces Europe.

80. *Pontus . . . Mysia*: All provinces now in Turkey.

81. *Amazons*: Warlike women who lived in Pontus.

82. *Medes*: Media is now basically Iraq.

83. *Hyrcanians*: Hyrcania is now part of Iran.

84. *Parthians*: A Scythian people occupying the Khurasan region of Iran.

85. *Carmanians*: Carmana, now Kerman, is a part of Iran on the Persian Gulf.

86. *Aria*: A Persian province now in Afghanistan.

87. *Paropamisus*: A high mountain beyond the Caspian Sea, now called the Hindu Kush.

88. *Drangiana*: Land of a Persian or Bactrian tribe in Iran and Afghanistan.

89. *Gedrosia*: Country now in Iran and Pakistan.

90. *human flesh*: "We have already said that among the Scythians there are many peoples who live on human flesh. . . . Beyond the Alps they had the custom of sacrificing people, which is little different from eating them." Pliny, in Hernández, *Historia natural*, f.8.

91. *griffins*: Fabulous beasts, half lion and half eagle.

92. *Mount Imaus*: The Himalayas.

93. *Sciapodes*: "They say that in Ethiopia there exists the people called Sciapodes, endowed with extraordinary legs and great speed. The Greeks call them Skiopodai because in the summer, lying face-up on the ground, they shade themselves with the enormous size of their feet." Isidoro, *Etimologías*, 2:51.

94. *without mouths or eyes*: "Others have such a small mouth that they can only ingest food making use of the small hole in an oat stalk." Isidoro, *Etimologías*, 2:51.

95. *upper lip*: "Others exhibit such a prominent lower lip that when they sleep they cover their whole face with it to protect themselves from the sun." Isidoro, *Etimologías*, 2:51.

96. *Island of Paria*: There is a Paria peninsula in Venezuela.

97. *Isabella*: Probably an error for Hispaniola.

98. *Santa Marta*: On the coast of Colombia.

99. *New Spain*: Mexico.

100. *the land of codfish*: Nova Scotia. F has, instead, "the Land of Prester John."

101. *invincible*: F has, instead, "unspeakable."

102. *scab*: the following word is indecipherable in the manuscripts.

103. *different in appearance*: both A and F offer the illogical reading of "similar in appearance."

104. This heading and the remainder of chapter 9 are not in A but have been taken from K.

105. *earthly death*: the reading of F; K has "eternal death."

106. *Now some . . . not correct*: The reading of F; A has the illogical "and they told me they are dispersed in mixtures and compounds, and they told me it was not so."

107. *eastern peoples*: the reading of F; A has "horizons."

108. *9,280 leagues*: the figures of this sort vary widely in the copies of *Face of the Earth*. I have reproduced those appearing in A for the first heaven, those in K for the other heavens.

109. *a marvel of a bird*: "The storks . . . , heralds of spring, who love to be with other storks, enemies of snakes, fly across the seas and, forming flocks, migrate to Asia. . . . The affection they feel for their young is something to see. They care for their nest so faithfully and incubate the eggs so long they come to lose their feathers. . . ." Isidoro, *Etimologías*, 2:109.

110. *the unicorn*: The description given by Pliny does not include the specific version of the legend mentioned by Sor María, though there is a similarity. "Some people have believed that its horn is beneficial against poison and other ills, taking for a fact that it is the same as the ass to which the aforesaid powers are attributed, for Aelianus, in the fourth book, chapter fifty-one, says that the horn of the East-Indian ass, when drunk, protects against the incurable diseases of spasm, coral gout and poisoning." In Hernández, *Historia natural*, 1:382.

111. *matroquillo*: Hernandez's version of Pliny includes the following: "When this animal, then, has eaten its fill of fish and, with its mouth dirty from the food that has stuck to it, while sleeping on the river bank, a little bird called there a *trochilo* and, in Italy, the king of the birds, stimulates and invites it to open its mouth, cleaning first some parts and then others for the purpose of its own nourishment, and then the teeth and in the throat. While they are lying there with their mouths wide open, enjoying the sweetness of being scratched this way, the ichneumon sees that they are immersed in pleasure and, quick as an arrow, goes in the mouth and eats right through the guts." Hernandez comments: "It cleans the teeth of the crocodile and lives off the filth that it removes and the leeches that are stuck to the throat; then, moved by natural benevolence wakes it so that it may avoid the injury caused by the ichneumon." 1:386–87, 88.

112. *most high*: the reading of F; A has "amazing."

113. *properties of eagles*: "They tell, too, that it looks straight at the sun without closing its eyes and for that reason seizes its chicks in its claws and holds them up to the sun's rays, judging them worthy of their species if they hold their gaze steady; on the other hand, the ones that blink are abandoned as unworthy of their species." Isidoro, *Etimologías*, 2:107.

114. *a remarkable property*: "Cranes owe their name to the sound of their voice. . . . At night they take turns with sentry duty and keep watch on a set schedule. In one of their claws they hold small pebbles, to drive away sleep. The sound of the stones falling warns them to pay attention." Isidoro, *Etimologías*, 2:107–9.

115. Misnumbering probably due to scribal error.

116. A does not have a heading for "First Heaven"; "Second Heaven" and the remainder of chapter 15 are from K.

Chapter 4

1. Kendrick, *Mary of Agreda*, chapter 2.

2. Joaquín Pérez Villanueva, president of the Center for Inquisition Studies, has analyzed the circumstances of this investigation by the Holy Office; see *Sor María y Felipe IV*, p. 384.

3. On Benavides' character, see the third chapter in Kendrick, *Mary of Agreda*, and the editorial notes by Hodge, Hammond, and Rey in Benavides, *Fray Alonso*.

4. A recent study by Pérez Villanueva brings to light and analyzes documents that reveal the extent and nature of this inter-order controversy. See his "Algo más sobre la Inquisición y Sor María de Agreda: la prodigiosa evangelización americana."

5. In commenting on a striking case of Spanish explorers including Indian mythology in their report as a justification for another expedition, I have researched the question and referred to other relevant studies. See Clark Colahan and Alfred Rodriguez, "Relación de Fray Francisco de Escobar del viaje desde el Reino de Nuevo México hasta el Mar del Sur."

6. Kessell, "Ministry to the Jumanos," p. 13.

7. Weber, *Teresa of Avila*, p. 35.

8. Franco, *Plotting Women*, p. 22.

9. Arenal and Schlau, *Untold Sisters*, p. 191.

10. Franco, *Plotting Women*, p. 16.

11. On the myth of the hero and its application to Teresa de Avila, see Vázquez Fernández, *Una lectura de Santa Teresa*, pp. 60–61.

12. Cited in Kessell, "Ministry to the Jumanos," p. 23.

13. See the thorough handbook on the subject by Janet Lee Mitchell, *Out-of-body Experiences*.

14. Benavides, *Fray Alonso*, pp. 92–96, 136–49. In using the names of the documents as chapter subheadings, I have shortened and adapted them so that they conform to the style of the other subheadings in this study. Otherwise, the letters and reports in this chapter, with the exception of the report to Father Manero, appear as translated by Hodge, Hammond, and Rey in the 1940s.

15. Serrano y Sanz, *Apuntes*, 1:594–95.

16. *four copies*: See the description by Serrano y Sanz, *Apuntes*, 1:594.

17. *mandavit de te*: the reading of R; O omits "de te"; Sor María's approximate citation by memory is of Psalms 91:11: "For He will give his angels charge of you to guard you in all your ways."

18. *his angels*: the reading of R; O has "six angels."

Chapter 5

1. MS F, folio 4.
2. Holbrook, "Margery Kempe," p. 29.
3. Arenal and Schlau, *Untold Sisters*, p. 197.
4. Holbrook, "Margery Kempe," p. 33.
5. Pérez Villanueva, *Felipe IV*, p. 19.
6. Esposito, *La mística ciudad*, p. 32.
7. Holbrook, "Margery Kempe," p. 32.
8. Weber, *Teresa of Avila*, p. 11.
9. Coleman, *English Mystics*, p. 156.
10. Arenal and Schlau, *Untold Sisters*, p. 14.
11. Ibid., pp. 242–43.
12. See their description in Serrano y Sanz, 1:595–96.
13. "My beloved is to me a bag of myrrh, that lies between my breasts." Song of Songs, 1:13.
14. Isaiah, 14:13–14.
15. The contrast is between the rod of iron that, according to Revelation 2:27, will rule the strict justice of the final judgment and the rod used by Moses to take water from the rock of Moreb in the desert, as recounted in Exodus 17.
16. The last paragraph has been taken from F. Q has "Up to here is all that was found by the venerable mother in this case."

Chapter 6

1. Seco Serrano, *Cartas*, 109:222–24.
2. Arraj, *St. John*, p. 57.

3. Holbrook, "Margery Kempe," p. 33.

4. Coleman, *English Mystics*, p. 157.

5. Warner, *Alone of All Her Sex*, p. 337.

6. McEntire, "Doctrine of Compunction," p. 77.

7. Dickman, *English Devotional Tradition*, p. 161.

8. Weber, *Teresa of Avila*, p. 75.

9. Arenal and Schlau, *Untold Sisters*, p. 152.

10. Cited in Arraj, *St. John*, p. 149.

11. See Solaguren's "Introducción" in Agreda, *Mística ciudad*, pp. xxx–xxxi.

12. Genesis, chapters 29 and 30, tells how Jacob served Laban seven years in order to marry Rachel, then was given, instead, her older sister, Leah. The latter bore him several children, however, while Rachael, whom he married later, bore only Joseph.

13. Eliade, *Cosmos and History*, p. 11.

14. Weber, *Teresa of Avila*, p. 50.

15. Chapter 14 of the Second Part of his *Guide for Sinners* is entitled "Regarding the third privilege of virtue, which is the light and supernatural knowledge that our Lord gives to the virtuous." Granada, *Obras*, 1:198.

16. Ibid., pp. 124–25.

17. Calvert, "Osuna's Meditations," p. 6.

18. Granada, *Obras*, vols. 6 and 8.

19. Granada, *Obras*, 8:89.

20. Wilson, *Spanish and English Literature*, pp. 236–37.

21. Dickman, *English Devotional Tradition*, pp. 156–57.

22. Coleman, *English Mystics*, pp. 175–76.

23. Kempe, *The Book*, pp. 11–12.

24. Swietlicki, *Spanish Christian Cabala*, p. 69, n. 88.

25. Weissman, *The Midrash*, p. vii.

26. Swietlicki, *Spanish Christian Cabala*, p. 9.

27. Ibid., p. 83.

28. Eliade, *Cosmos and History*, p. 23.

29. Agreda, *Mística ciudad*, pp. 349–87.

30. Hatzfeld (*Mística española*, pp. 227–34) stresses the fundamental importance of the Song of Songs for the Spanish mystical tradition. A broader treatment can be found in Dorothy H. Donnelly's essay "The Sexual Mystic: Embodied Spirituality."

31. Agreda, *Mística ciudad*, book 2, chapter 2.

32. Many editions of the *Mística ciudad*, including the 1970 one cited, foot-

note the biblical phrases embedded in the text. That edition shows fifteen quotations from the Song of Songs in the nine chapters under discussion, with three in chapter 8 alone.

33. Kempe, *The Book*, p. 75.

34. Catherine of Siena, *The Dialogue*, p. 126.

35. Granada, *Obras*, 1:113.

36. Agreda, *Mística ciudad*, p. 386.

37. Cited in Arraj, *St. John*, pp. 53–54.

38. Granada, *Obras*, 8:41.

39. Holbrook, "Margery Kempe," p. 33.

40. Eliade, *Cosmos and History*, pp. 10–11.

41. Franz, "Individuation," p. 213.

42. Warner, *Alone of All Her Sex*, pp. 93–94.

43. Cervantes, *Persiles and Sigismunda*, pp. 220–22.

44. Cited in Eliade, *Cosmos and History*, p. 8.

45. Revelation 21:2ff.

46. Arenal and Schlau, *Untold Sisters*, p. 199.

47. Dickman, "Margery Kempe and the English Devotional Tradition," p. 158.

48. Fox, *The Coming of the Cosmic Christ*.

Select Bibliography

Agreda, María de Jesús de. *Mística ciudad de Dios: Vida de la Virgen María.* Madrid: Fareso, 1970.

Agustine. *La ciudad de Dios.* 2 vols. José Moran, trans. Madrid: Biblioteca de Autores Cristianos, 1964.

Alphraganus. *Brevis ac Perutilis Compilatio Alfragani Astro-nomorum Peritissimi Totum ad Continens quod ad Rudimenta Astronomica Est Opportunum.* Johannes Hispalenses, trans. Ferrara, 1493.

Amatora, Mary. "Marian Masterpiece for Our Times." *The Age of Mary* 5, no. 1 (Jan.–Feb. 1958): 9–13.

Apiano, Pedro. *Libro de la cosmografía, el qual trata la descripción del miundo y sus partes, por muy claro y lindo artificio, augumentado por el doctissimo varon Gemma Frisio, doctor en medecina, y mathematico excellentissimo: con otros dos libros del dicho Gemma, de la materia mesma. Agora nuevamente traduzidos en romance castellano.* Antwerp, 1575.

Arenal, Electa. "The Convent as Catalyst for Autonomy: Two Hispanic Nuns of the Seventeenth Century." In *Women in Hispanic Literature: Icons and Fallen Idols.* Beth Miller, ed., 147–83. Berkeley: University of California Press, 1983.

———. "This life within me won't keep still." In *Reinventing the Americas: Comparative Studies of Literature of the United States and Spanish America.* Bell Gale Chevigny and Gari Laguardia, eds., 158–202. Cambridge: Cambridge University Press, 1986.

Arenal, Electa, and Stacey Schlau. *Untold Sisters: Hispanic Nuns in Their Own Works.* Albuquerque: University of New Mexico Press, 1989.

Arraj, James. *St. John of the Cross and Dr. C. G. Jung: Christian Mysticism in the Light of Jungian Psychology*. Chiloquin, Oregon: Tools for Inner Growth, 1986.

Benavides, Alonso. *Fray Alonso de Benavides' Revised Memorial of 1634*. Frederick Webb Hodge, George P. Hammond, and Agapito Rey, eds. Albuquerque: University of New Mexico Press, 1945.

———. "Memorial . . . a la Majestad del rey don Felipe Quarto . . . . Hecho por fray Alonso de Benavides, 1630." In *Documentos para servir a la historia del Nuevo Mexico 1538–1778*, 1–77. Madrid: Porrúa Turanzas, 1962.

———. "Tanto que se sacó de una carta. . . ." In Francisco Palou, *Evangelista del Mar Pacifico: fray Junipero Serra*, 308–17. 1787; reprinted Madrid: Aguilar, 1944.

Calvert, Laura. "Osuna's Meditations: Between Preaching and Poetry." *Studia Mystica* 11, no. 3 (fall 1988): 7–14.

Carrico, James. *The Life of Venerable Mary of Agreda*. Stockbridge, Massachusetts: Marian Fathers, 1959.

Castañeda, Carlos E. "The Woman in Blue." *The Age of Mary* 5, no. 1 (Jan.–Feb. 1958): 28–29.

Catherine of Siena. *The Dialogue*. Suzanne Noffke, trans. New York: Paulist Press, 1980.

"The Catholic Reformation in Education Lies Within the Four Volumes of *The Mystical City of God*." *The Age of Mary* 5, no. 1 (Jan.–Feb. 1958): 73–75.

Cervantes, Miguel de. *The Trials of Persiles and Sigismunda, a Northern Story*. Celia Weller and Clark Colahan, trans. Berkeley: University of California Press, 1989.

Clavius, Cristobal. *In Sphaeram Joannis de Sacro Bosco Commentarius*. Rome, 1570.

Colahan, Clark, and Alfred Rodriguez. "A New México *Alabado* about María de Jesús de Agreda." *The Liberal and Fine Arts Review* 5 (1985): 4–14.

———. "Relación de Fray Francisco de Escobar del viaje desde el Reino de Nuevo México hasta el Mar del Sur." *Missionalia Hispanica* 43 (1986): 373–94.

Colahan, Clark, and Celia Weller. "An Angelic Epilogue," *Studia Mystica* 13 (1990): 50–59.

Coleman, T. W. *English Mystics of the Fourteenth Century*. 1938; reprinted Westport, Connecticut: Greenwood, 1971.

Conde, María José. "La M. Patrocinio de las Llagas en la literatura española contemporánea (Benito Pérez Galdós y Ramón del Valle Inclán)." Unpublished paper presented at the Primer Congreso Internacional de la Orden Concepcionista, 1489–1989. León, Spain, 1990.

Cordero Cuevas, Idalia. *El "Buscón" o la verguenza de Pablos y la ira de don Francisco.* Madrid: Playor, 1987.

Dickman, Susan. "Margery Kempe and the English Devotional Tradition." In *The Medieval Mystical Tradition in England: Papers read at the Exeter Symposium, July 1980.* Marion Glasscoe, ed., 156–72. University of Exeter, 1980.

Donnelly, Dorothy H. "The Sexual Mystic: Embodied Spirituality." In *The Feminist Mystic and Other Essays on Women and Spirituality.* Mary Giles, ed., 120–41. New York: Crossroad, 1985.

Duhem, Pierre. *Le système du monde: histoire des doctrines cosmologiques.* 5 vols. Paris: Hermann, 1913–15.

Eliade, Mircea. *Cosmos and History: The Myth of the Eternal Return.* Willard R. Trask, trans. New York: Harper, 1959.

Esposito, Augustine M., Rev., O.S.A. *La mística ciudad de Dios (1670): Sor María de Jesús de Agreda.* Potomac: Scripta Humanistica, 1990.

Esteve-Barba, Francisco. *Biblioteca pública de Toledo: catálogo de la colección de manuscritos Borbon-Lorenzana.* Madrid: Gongora, 1942.

Forcione, Alban K. *Aristotle, Cervantes and the Persiles.* Princeton: Princeton University Press, 1972.

Fox, Matthew. *The Coming of the Cosmic Christ: The Healing of Mother Earth and the Birth of a Global Renaissance.* San Francisco: Harper and Row, 1988.

Franco, Jean. *Plotting Women: Gender and Representation in Mexico.* New York: Columbia University Press, 1989.

Franz, M.-L. von. "The process of individuation." In *Man and His Symbols,* 158–229. New York: Doubleday, 1976.

"George J. Blatter . . . Fiscar Marison . . . Louis W. Bernicken . . . Three Great Names in U.S. Agredana." *Age of Mary* 5, no. 1 (Jan.–Feb. 1958): 9–13.

Giles, Mary E. *The Book of Prayer of Sor María of Santo Domingo, a Study and Translation.* Albany: State University of New York Press, 1990.

Granada, Fray Luis de. *Obras.* Madrid, 1786.

Gumbinger, Cuthbert. "Father Solanus Casey, Capuchin Agreda Devotee." *Age of Mary* 5, no. 1 (Jan.–Feb. 1958): 105–7.

Hallenbeck, Cleve, and Juanita H. Williams. *Legends of the Spanish Southwest.* Glendale, California: Arthur Clark, 1938.

Hatzfeld, Helmut. *Estudios literarios sobre mística española*. 3d ed., Madrid: Gredos, 1976.

Hera y de la Varra, Bartholomé Balentín de la. *Repertorio del mundo particular de las spheras del cielo y orbes elementales* . . . Madrid, 1584.

Hernández, Francisco. *Historia natural de Cayo Plinio Segundo*. 3 vols. 1624; reprinted, Mexico: Universidad Nacional de México, 1966.

Holbrook, Sue Ellen. "Margery Kempe and Wynkyn de Worde." In *The Medieval Mystical Tradition in England: Exeter Symposium IV*. Marion Glasscoe, ed., 27–46. Cambridge: D.S. Brewer, 1987.

Ioannis de Toledo. *Cursos Theologicus*. 3 vols. León, 1672.

Isidoro de Sevilla. *Etimologías*. 2 vols. Madrid: Biblioteca de Autores Cristianos, 1982.

Kempe, Margery. *The Book of Margery Kempe*. W. Butler-Bowdon, ed. New York: Devin-Adair, 1944.

Kendrick, T. D. *Mary of Agreda: The Life and Legend of a Spanish Nun*. London: Routledge and Kegan Paul, 1967.

Kessell, John L. "In Body, Spirit, or Not at All? María de Agreda's Ministry to the Jumanos of New Mexico in the 1620's." In *Mysteries of the Amerian West*, forthcoming.

López Piñero, José María. *Ciencia y técnica en la sociedad española de los siglos XVI y XVII*. Barcelona: Labor Universitaria, 1979.

Márquez Villanueva, Francisco. "Los inventos de San Juan de Avila." Vol. 3, *Homenaje al Profesor Carriazo*, Seville: Universidad de Sevilla, 1973.

——— "Sobre la occidentalidad cultural de España." In *Relecciónes de literatura medieval*, 135–68. Seville: Universidad de Sevilla, 1977.

Maurolico, Francisco. *Cosmographia in Tres Diálogos Distinta*. Venice, 1561.

McEntire, Sandra. "The Doctrine of Compunction from Bede to Margery Kempe." In *Medieval Mystical Tradition in England: Exeter Symposium IV*. Marion Glasscoe, ed., 77–90. Cambridge: D. S. Brewer, 1987.

McKendrick, Melveena. *Woman and Society in the Spanish Drama of the Golden Age: A Study of the* Mujer Varonil. Cambridge: Cambridge University Press, 1974.

Medina, Pedro de. *Libro de la verdad* in *Obras*. Angel González Palencia, ed. Madrid: C.S.I.C., 1944.

———. *Suma de cosmographía*. Juan Fernández Jiménez, ed. Valencia: Hispanófila, 1980.

Mitchell, Janet Lee. *Out-of-body Experiences*. New York: Ballantine, 1981.

New Catholic Encyclopedia. New York: McGraw Hill, 1967–1989.

Omaechevarría, Ignacio, "La Madre Agreda entre los indios de Texas." *Celtiberia* 29 (1965): 7–22.

————. "Sor María de Jesús de Agreda y la devoción de la divina Peregrina." *Archivo Ibero-Americano* 27 (1967): 219–27.

Ortroy, F. van. *Bibliographie de l'oeuvre de Pierre Apian*. Amsterdam, 1963.

Palou, Francisco. *Palou's Life of Fray Junípero Serra*. Trans. and notes by Maynard J. Geiger. Washington, D.C.: Academy of American Franciscan History, 1955.

Pérez Rioja, José Antonio. *Proyección de la Venerable María de Agreda (Ensayo para una bibliografía de fuentes impresas)*. Soria: Centro de Estudios Sorianos, 1965.

Pérez Villanueva, Joaquín. "Algo mas sobre la Inquisición y Sor María de Agreda: la prodigiosa evangelización americana." *Hispania Sacra* 37 (1985): 585–618.

————. *Felipe IV y Luisa Enríquez Manrique de Lara, Condesa de Paredes de Nava: Un epistolario inédito*. Salamanca: Caja de Ahorros, 1986.

————. *Sor María de Agreda y Felipe IV: un epistolario en su tiempo* in *Historia de la Iglesia en España*. 5 vols. Madrid: Biblioteca de Autores Cristianos, 1979.

Perry, T. A. *The Moral Proverbs of Santob de Carrión: Jewish Wisdom in Christian Spain*. Princeton, New Jersey: Princeton University Press, 1987.

Raizizun, May. "The Blue Lady." *New Mexico Magazine* 40 (Feb. 1962): 22 ff.

Ranke-Heinemann, Uta. *Eunuchs for the Kingdom of Heaven: Women, Sexuality and the Catholic Church*. Peter Heinegg, trans. New York: Penguin, 1990.

Robe, Stanley L. *Hispanic Legends from New Mexico*. Vol. 31, Folklore and Mythology Studies, 531–32. Berkeley: University of California, 1980.

Rossi, Rosa. *Teresa de Avila: biografía de una escritora*. Marieta Gargatagli, trans. Barcelona: Icaria, 1984.

Seco Serrano, Carlos. *Cartas de sor María de Jesús de Agreda y de Felipe IV*. Biblioteca de Autores Españoles, vols. 108–09. Madrid: Atlas, 1958.

Serra, Junípero. *Writings of Junipero Serra*. Antonine Tibesar, ed. Vol. 1. Washington, D.C.: Academy of American Franciscan History, 1955.

Serrano y Sanz, Manuel. *Apuntes para una biblioteca de escritoras españolas desde el año 1401 al 1833*. Madrid, 1903–1905.

Silverman, Joseph. Review of Swietlicki, *Spanish Christian Cabala*. In *Studia Mystica* 11, no. 3 (fall 1988): 70.

Smith, Craig. "Visions of Sister María." *Santa Fe Reporter*, Jan. 8, 1986.

Swietlicki, Catherine. *Spanish Christian Cabala: The Works of Luis de León, Santa Teresa de Jesús, and San Juan de la Cruz*. Columbia: University of Missouri Press, 1986.

Teresa de Avila. *Las moradas*. Madrid: Espasa-Calpe, 1962.

Torrance, Betty M. "Selections from the *Audi, Filia*, I and II." *Studia Mystica* 11, no. 3 (fall 1988): 21–30.

Uribe, Angel. "Fondo Agredano de la Biblioteca de Aránzazu." *Archivo Ibero-Americano* 27 (1967): 249–304.

Vázquez Fernández, Antonio. *Notas para una lectura de las "Moradas" de Santa Teresa desde la psicología profunda*. Salamanca: Universidad Pontificia, 1982.

Venegas, Alejo. *Declaración de la diferencia de libros que ay en el universo, a saber libro original o divino, libro racional y revelación*. Toledo, 1540.

Warner, Marina. *Alone of All Her Sex: The Myth and the Cult of the Virgin Mary*. New York: Knopf, 1976.

Weber, Alison. *Teresa of Avila and the Rhetoric of Femininity*. Princeton: Princeton University Press, 1990.

Weissman, Moshe. *The Midrash Says*. New York: Benei Yakov Publications, 1980.

Wickers, Mary Amideus. "An Unpublished Manuscript on . . . The Lady in Blue." *Age of Mary* 5, no. 1 (Jan.–Feb. 1958): 105–7.

Wilson, Edward M. *Spanish and English Literature of the 16th and 17th Centuries*. London: Cambridge University Press, 1980.

Ximénez Samaniego, Joseph. *Prologo galeato. Relación de la vida de la venerable madre sor María de Jesús . . .* Madrid, 1721.

Zarco Cuevas, Julián. *Catálogo de los manuscritos castellanos de la real biblioteca de el Escorial*. 3 vols. Madrid: Helénica, 1924.

Index

About the Author

CLARK COLAHAN teaches Spanish language and literature and comparative medieval literature at Whitman College. He holds degrees from Pomona College, California State University at Los Angeles, and the University of New Mexico. Author of numerous articles in American, British, and Spanish journals on Renaissance literature, in 1989 he published, in collaboration with Celia Weller, an annotated translation of Cervantes' last book, *The Trials of Persiles and Sigismunda*. His 1994 study with Alfred Rodriguez, "Juan Maldonado and Lazarillo de Tormes," establishes at last a strong candidate for the authorship of the original picaresque novel. Two of his recent Cervantine studies, "Toward an Onomastics of Persiles/Periando and Sigismunda/Auristela" and "Lunar Pigs Trash Crazed Green Cultists (*DQ* 2, chapters 58–68)," explore Cervantes' use of Greek myth to invest female characters with power and autonomy.

Colahan's longstanding interest in Sor María de Agreda, which has taken him to convents and international conferences, has made him the scholarly world's leading "Agredista," and he played roles on and off camera in the 1993 documentary on Sor María by Spanish National Television.